PREFACE

The pieces in this book are from the Golden Age of song writing, including works by
George Gershwin, Cole Porter, Harold Arlen and Richard Rodgers among others.
These songs have stood the test of time to become 'standards' for jazz musicians as well as
singers; they represent the pinnacle of the art of melody writing, combining brilliant lyrics with
wonderful harmonies. But how to get started playing this wonderful repertoire?

This series aims to help aspiring jazz pianists (whether soloists, accompanists to singers
or instrumentalists, or pianists in a band or jazz group) to understand and get these
jazz standards firmly 'under their fingers'. Each piece is presented in two formats which gives
both the basic chord structure and symbols as well as a piano arrangement of each song.
By learning the changes, the chords will become familiar, the progressions more
readily understood and the shapes will lie comfortably under the hands. More information
on how to interpret and voice the chords is given on the following pages.

The first version of each song gives the melody, lyrics and chord symbols in its standard key[†].
Lyrics are given so that the character of the songs is understood. The chord symbols and basic
voicing of each chord helps players understand the structure and makes an ideal resource for
pianists who wish to play with singers, instrumentalists and jazz ensembles.
This format will ultimately give pianists the foundation on which to develop
personal interpretation and improvisation.

The arrangements for solo piano which follow keep largely to the same chord structure
and can again be used as the basis for further development and extemporisation.
These solos I have recorded on the accompanying downloadable audio.

I do recommend you listen to as many versions of these and other songs as possible,
not only by pianists but by singers and other instrumentalists. Recommended pianists must
include Oscar Peterson, George Shearing, Bill Evans, Art Tatum, André Previn and Keith Jarrett,
while singers should include Ella Fitzgerald, Frank Sinatra, Tony Bennett, Nat King Cole and
Michael Bublé. These vocalists are masters of phrasing and expression and not only perform
the melodies but the words themselves.

I wish to thank Thelma Johnson, David Sams and Gareth Bucket for their enthusiasm and
encouragement throughout the development of this series and in particular John Caudwell
for his expertise and advice in fine-tuning the chord section.

John Kember

[†] Standard keys are not only the keys that are generally associated with a particular song,
but those which are also compatible with the other instruments likely to make up the ensemble –
namely those in B♭ and E♭. This may explain the tendency to favour flat keys rather than sharp.

A GUIDE TO JAZZ CHORDS FOR PIANISTS

For a first approach, most pianists with a basic awareness of chords can figure out the notes required for a simple 8-chord sequence in C major, and may well interpret it as:

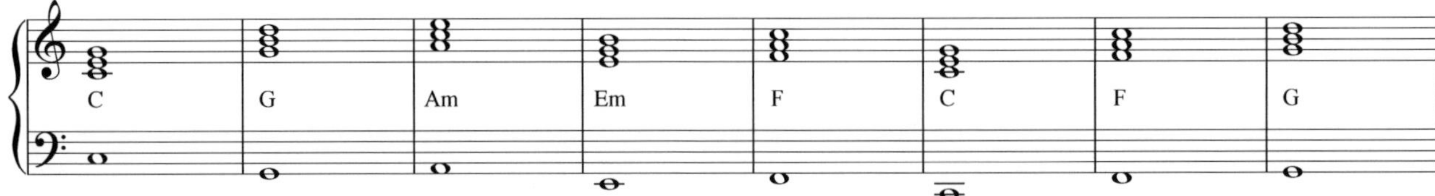

Not altogether musical, and breaking several rules of harmony, but given the advice to move the chord in contrary motion to the movement of the bass line, it may be somewhat improved. But what you need to 'see' is the hidden, smooth, stepwise movement the sequence offers:

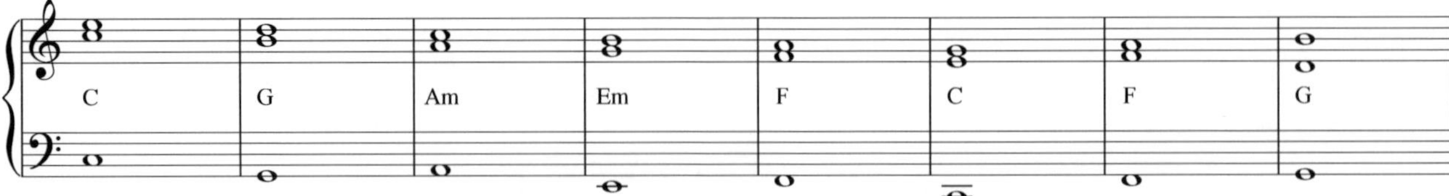

This sequence is now recognisable and demonstrates the skill required to make musical sense of the symbols. It involves learning how to voice the chords and link them as the composer intended, whilst keeping the player's own interpretation. Jazz pianists need to be able to negotiate their way through a sequence of seemingly unrelated chords as smoothly as possible and with minimum movement of upper parts, and in doing so find the (often chromatic) line.

GETTING TO KNOW THE CHORDS

Most chords are root based and are built upon the given note, adding 7th, 9th, 11th and 13th as required. Inversions of chords are shown as G/B (a G major chord over B in the bass). Similarly, F/C (F major chord over C) or E^7/B (E^7 chord over B).

- The first chords to master are the **sequence of 7ths**, a common progression found in many songs:

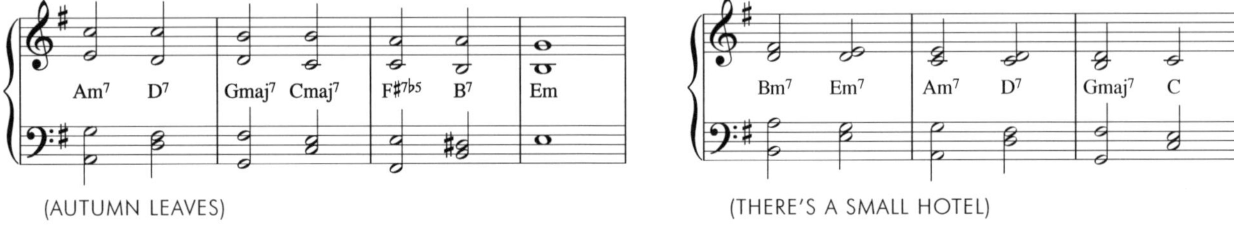

(AUTUMN LEAVES)　　　　(THERE'S A SMALL HOTEL)

George Gershwin – the master of harmony in this genre – takes the sequence and adds to it by augmenting the 5th ($B^{7\sharp5}$) or adding the 13th:

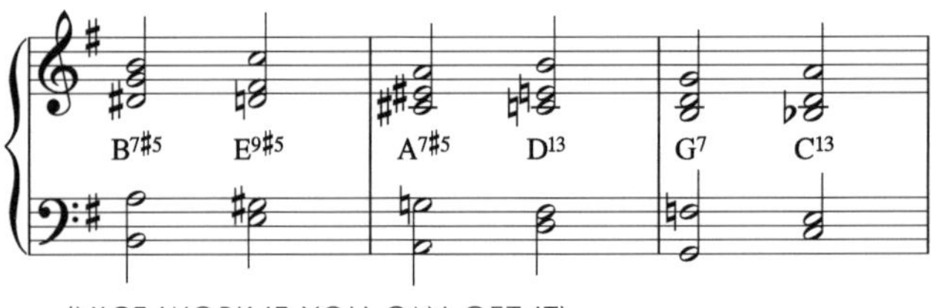

(NICE WORK IF YOU CAN GET IT)

- The **diminished 7th** is frequently used as part of a chromatic bass line, often between a root and 1st inversion chord. It can also be shown as D°.

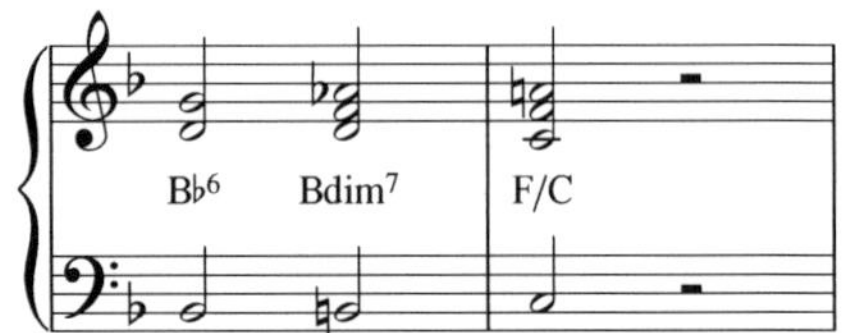

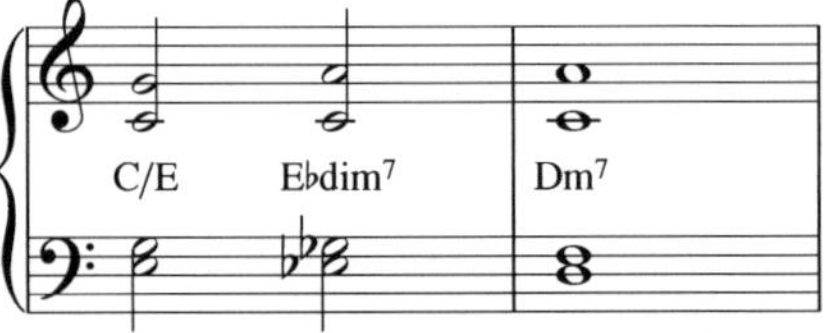

THE JAZZ PIANO PLAYER

STORMY WEATHER

...AND 15 OTHER CLASSIC JAZZ STANDARDS

ARRANGED AND PERFORMED BY JOHN KEMBER

Audio tracks are available to download by scanning the QR code
or going to fabermusic.com/audio.

CONTENTS

© 2008 by Faber Music Ltd
This edition first published in 2008
Brownlow Yard, 12 Roger Street, London WC1N 2JU
Music processed by Jackie Leigh
Cover design by Lydia Merrills-Ashcroft
Audio recorded and produced by Porcupine Studios
Printed in England by Caligraving Ltd
All rights reserved

ISBN10: 0-571-53156-3
EAN13: 978-0-571-53156-1

To buy Faber Music publications or to find out about the full range of titles available
please contact your local music retailer or Faber Music sales enquiries:

Faber Music Ltd, Burnt Mill, Elizabeth Way, Harlow CM20 2HX
Tel: +44 (0) 1279 82 89 82
fabermusic.com

- A chord which occurs frequently and is much easier to interpret than it looks is the **minor 7th chord with a flattened 5th**. Bm$^{7\flat5}$ is simply a D minor chord over B; or Em$^{7\flat5}$ is G minor over E. This chord can also be referred to as 'half-diminished' and indicated as $\varnothing$.

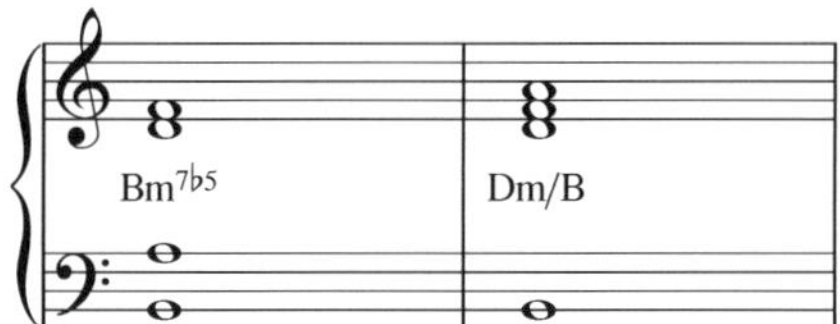

- The **suspended 4th** indicates a chord where the 4th is suspended which may or may not fall to the 3rd.

- As the name implies, the **major 7th** chord includes the 7th of the major key. So A^{maj7} would mean a G♯ (A^7 means a G♮).

- The **9th** gives added richness and 'crunch' to a chord. G^9 would generally imply both the 7th and the 9th, and like the 7th can be major or minor – so either a whole tone (2nd) above the root or a semitone (minor 2nd) above it (this is indicated as $^{\flat9}$). The addition of the 9th alone makes a good finishing chord.

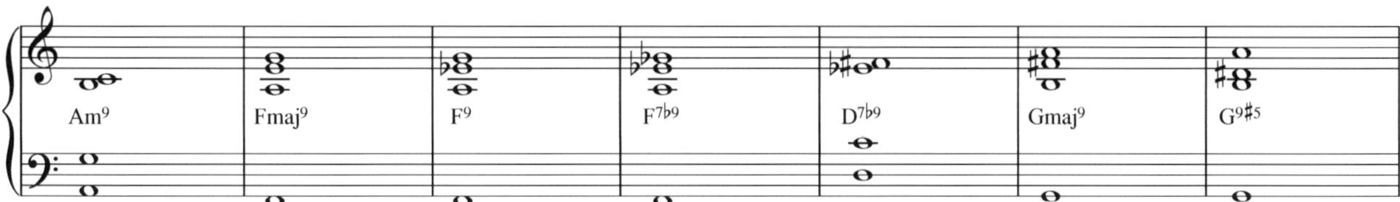

- The **11th** is used less often and usually omits the 3rd of the chord to avoid a clash. It can make a useful variation to the final cadence:

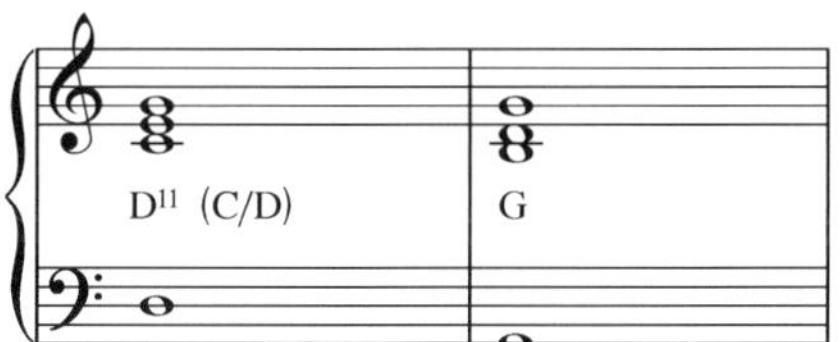

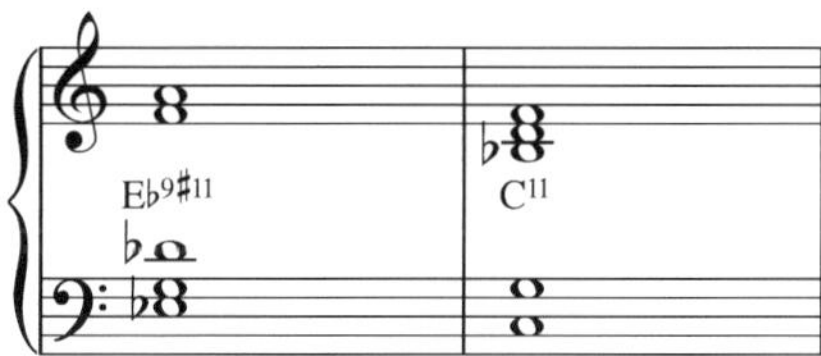

- The **13th** is sometimes indicated as G^{76} – the 13th above the root being the same as the 6th. The 13th does not mean that all 7 notes implied in the chord are to be played. It is best voiced as root, 3rd, 7th and 13th (6th). But of course other notes can be added as required.

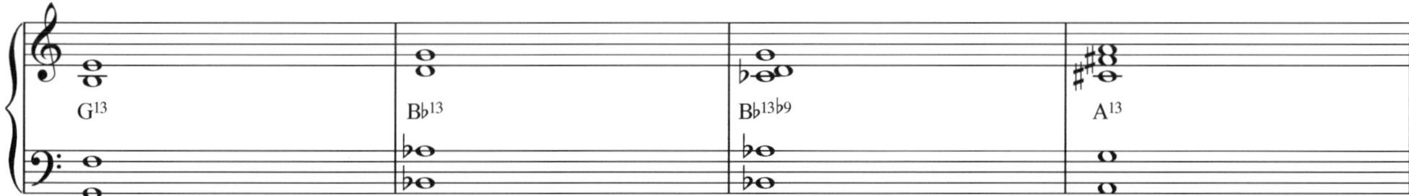

- The **6th** generally implies a first inversion feel to a chord, replacing the 5th for the 6th. At other times it is referred to as an 'added 6th' and uses both the 5th and 6th. This gives a very smooth, sugary texture to a final chord. In 'Summertime', Gershwin alternates Am^6 with E^7/B for the first four bars to spectacular effect.

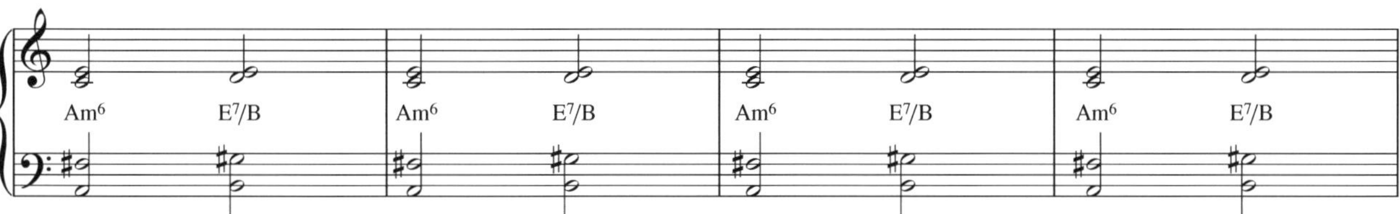

MY SHIP
(MELODY, LYRICS AND CHORD CHANGES)

Words by Ira Gershwin
Music by Kurt Weill

This music is copyright. Photocopying is illegal.

MY SHIP
(SOLO ARRANGEMENT)

OVER THE RAINBOW
(MELODY, LYRICS AND CHORD CHANGES)

Words by E Y Harburg
Music by Harold Arlen

18
Just a step be-yond the rain.
Some - where
Some - where
Bb9
Adim7/Bb
Fm7/Bb
Fm7
Bb13
Bb7
Eb
Cm7
22
o - ver the rain - bow, Way up high, There's a
o - ver the rain - bow Skies are blue, And the
Gm7
Eb7
Abmaj7
Bb13
Bb9#5
Gm7
C7b9
Fm7
Abm6
26
land that I heard of Once in a lul - la - by.
dreams that you dare to dream Real - ly do come true. Some
1.
2.
Ebmaj7
C7b9
Fm7
Bb7
Eb
Fm7
Bb7b9
Eb
Fm7
Bb7b9
30
day I'll wish up - on a star And wake up where the clouds are far be - hind me,
Ebmaj7
Fm7
Bb7
Gm11
C7

33
Where trou-bles melt like lem-on drops A - way a-bove the chim-ney tops That's
Fm7 Bb7 Ebmaj7 Am7b5 D7b9
36
where you'll find me. Some - where o - ver the rain - bow, Blue - birds
Gm7 Gbdim7 Fm7 Bb9 Eb6 Cm7 Gm7 Eb7 Abmaj7 Bb7sus
41
fly, Birds fly o - ver the rain-bow Why then, oh why can't I? If
Gm7 C7 Abmaj7 Db7 Ebmaj7 C7b9 Fm7 Bb7 Cm7 Abm6/Cb
46
hap-py lit - tle blue-birds fly Be - yond the rain-bow Why, oh why can't I?
Ebmaj7 Cm7 Fm7 Ab/Bb Fm7 Bb11b9 Eb69

OVER THE RAINBOW
(SOLO ARRANGEMENT)

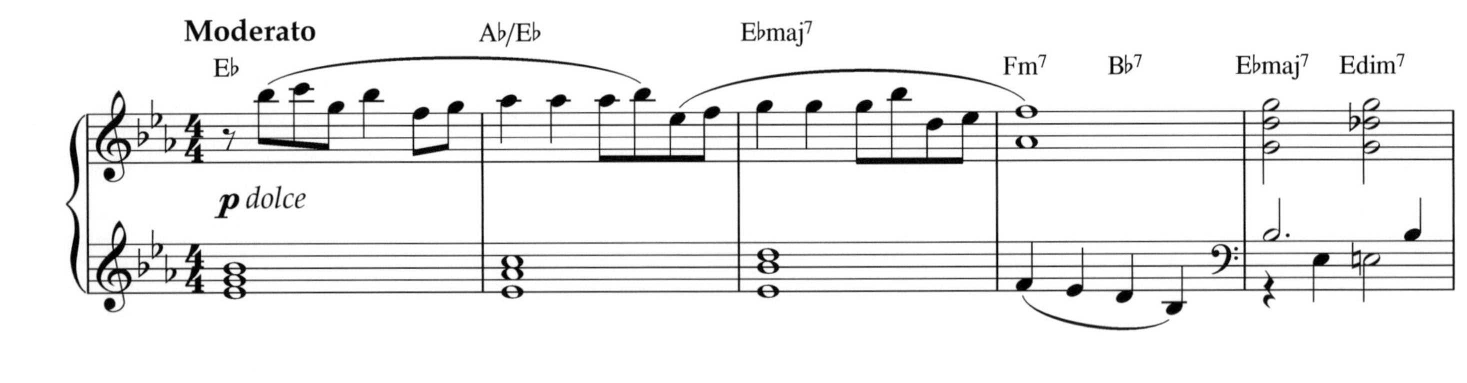

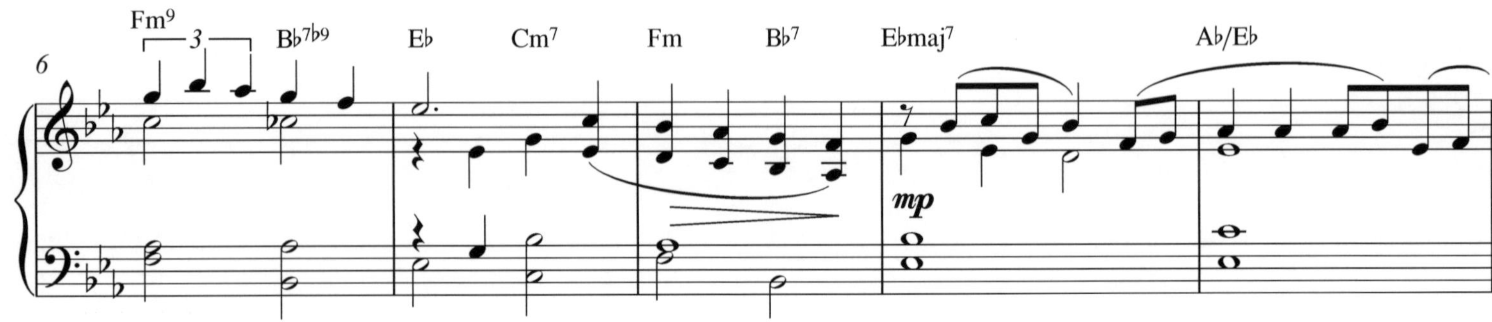

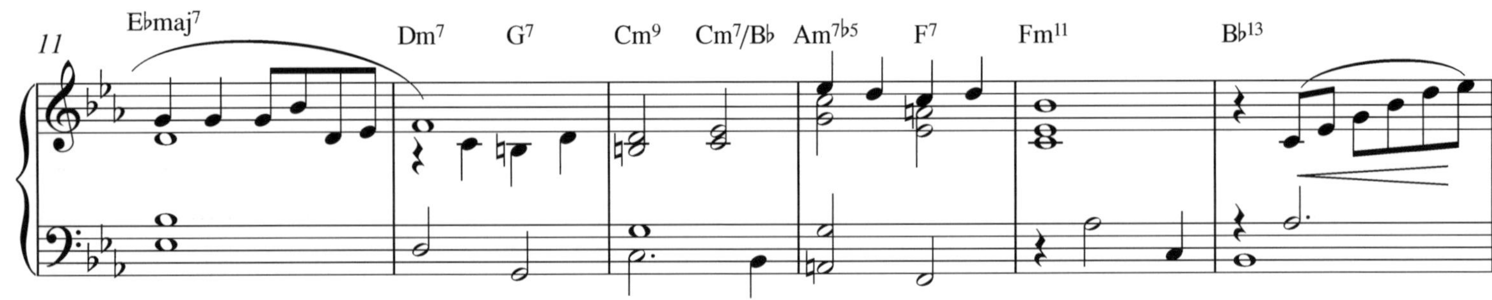

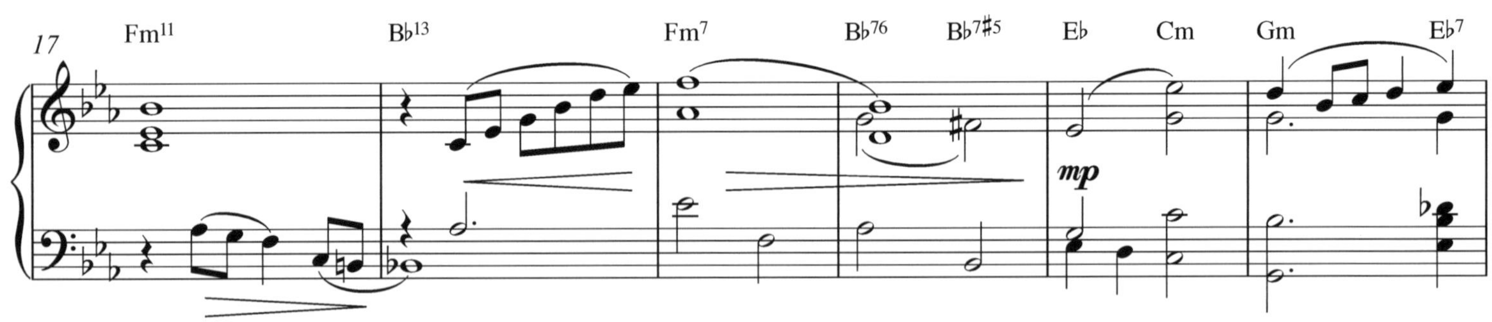

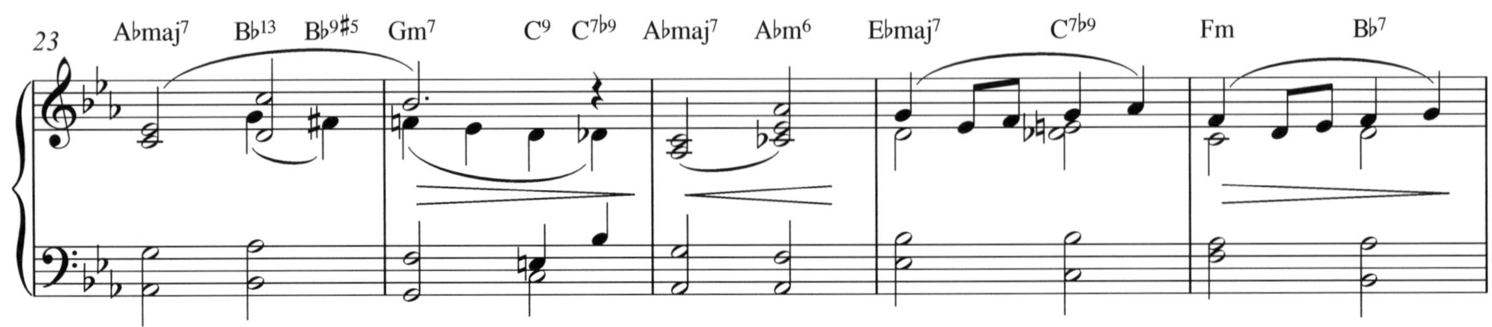

Eb Fm9 Bb7b9 Eb Cm Gm Eb7 Abmaj7 Bb11 Gm7 C7b9
p mf p
Abmaj7 Abm6 Eb C7b9 Fm Bb7 Eb
Ebmaj7 Ab/Eb Gm11 C7 Fm7 Bb7 Ebmaj7
p
Am7b5 D7b9 Gm Gbdim7 Fm Bb13 Bb9#5 Eb6 Cm Gm Eb7
f mp
Ab Bb13 Bb9#5 Gm7 C9 C-9 Abmaj7 Abm6 Ebmaj7 C7 C7b9b13 Fm Bb7sus Bb13 Cm
p
Ebmaj7 Fm7 Bb7 Cb Abm Eb6 (L.H.)

THERE'S A SMALL HOTEL

(MELODY, LYRICS AND CHORD CHANGES)

Words by Lorenz Hart
Music by Richard Rodgers

Not a sign of peo - ple — who wants peo - ple? When the
Cmaj7 Bm7b5 E7 E7b9 Am7 Am7b5 D7 Gmaj7 G6
stee - ple bell says "Good - night, sleep well," We'll thank that small ho - tel to -
Gmaj7 G6 Gmaj7 C9 Bm7 A#dim7 Am7 G#dim7 Am7 D7
1.
- ge - ther. thank that small ho - tel We'll creep in - to our lit - tle
G6 Am7 D7 Am7 D7 Bbmaj7
2.
shell And we will thank that small ho - tel to - ge - ther.
Cm7 F7 Gmaj7 Am7 D7 Gmaj7

THERE'S A SMALL HOTEL

(SOLO ARRANGEMENT)

A FOGGY DAY
(MELODY, LYRICS AND CHORD CHANGES)

Words and Music by
George Gershwin and Ira Gershwin

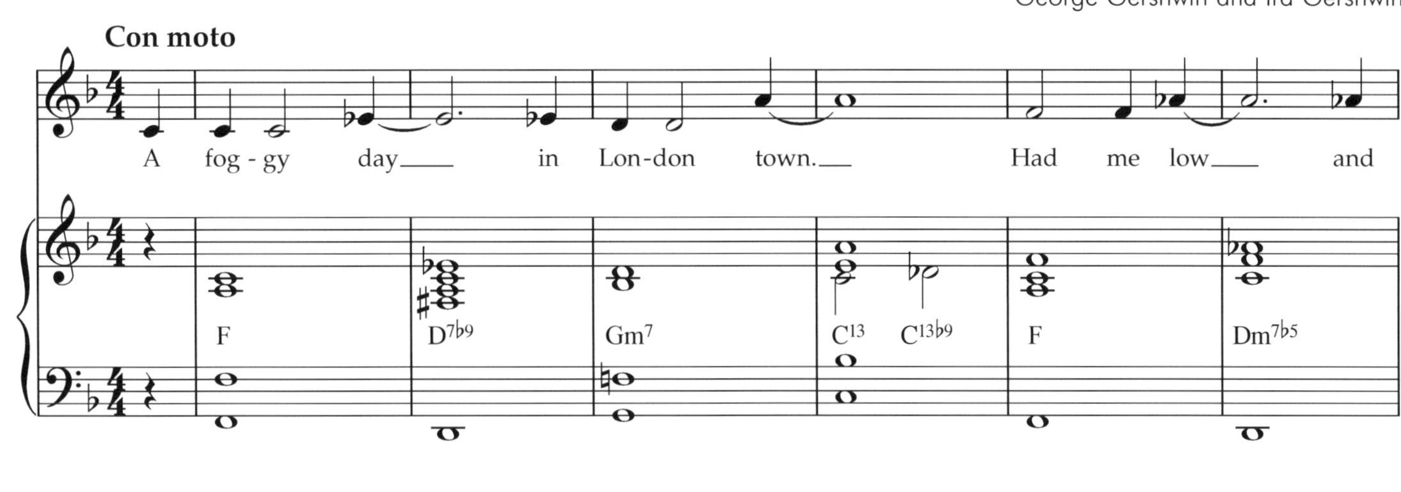

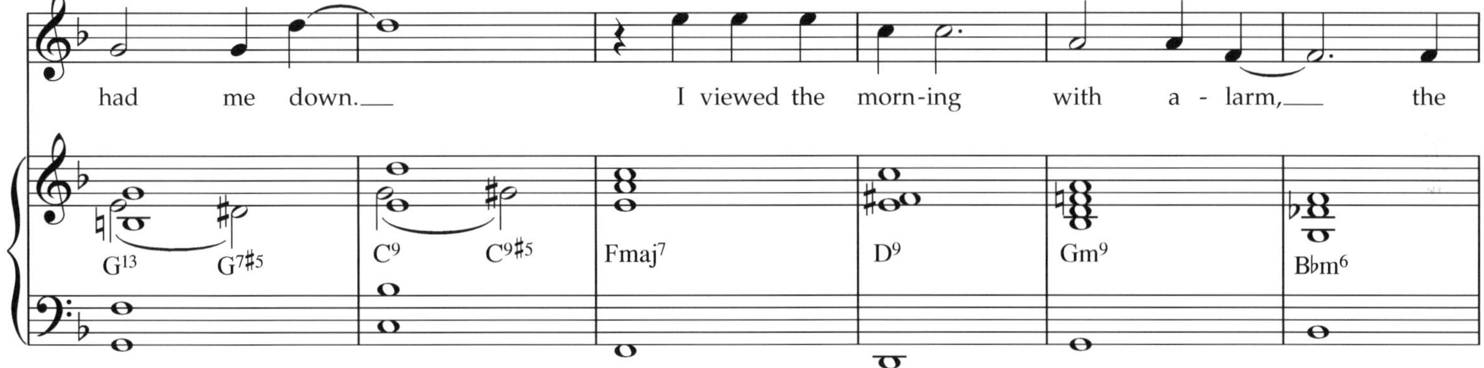

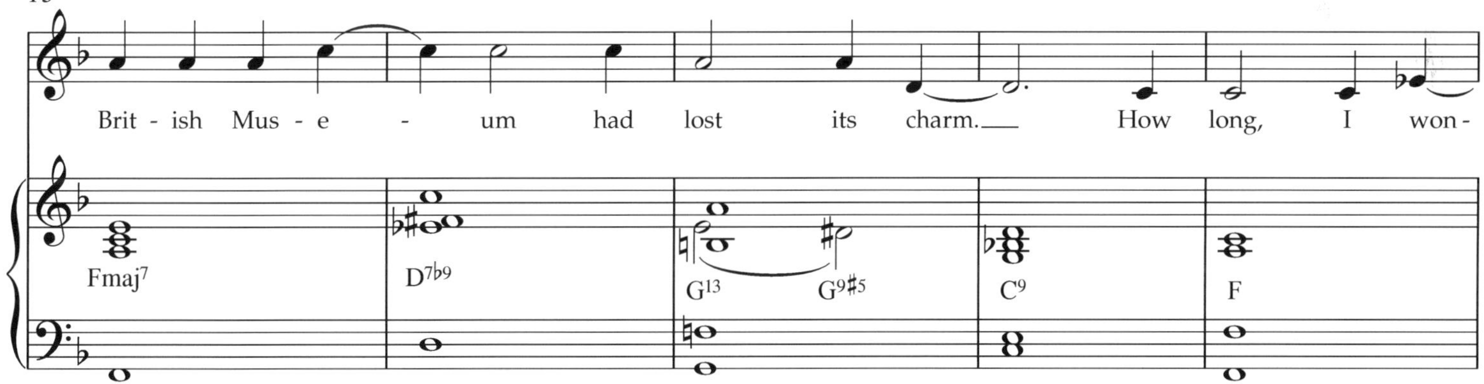

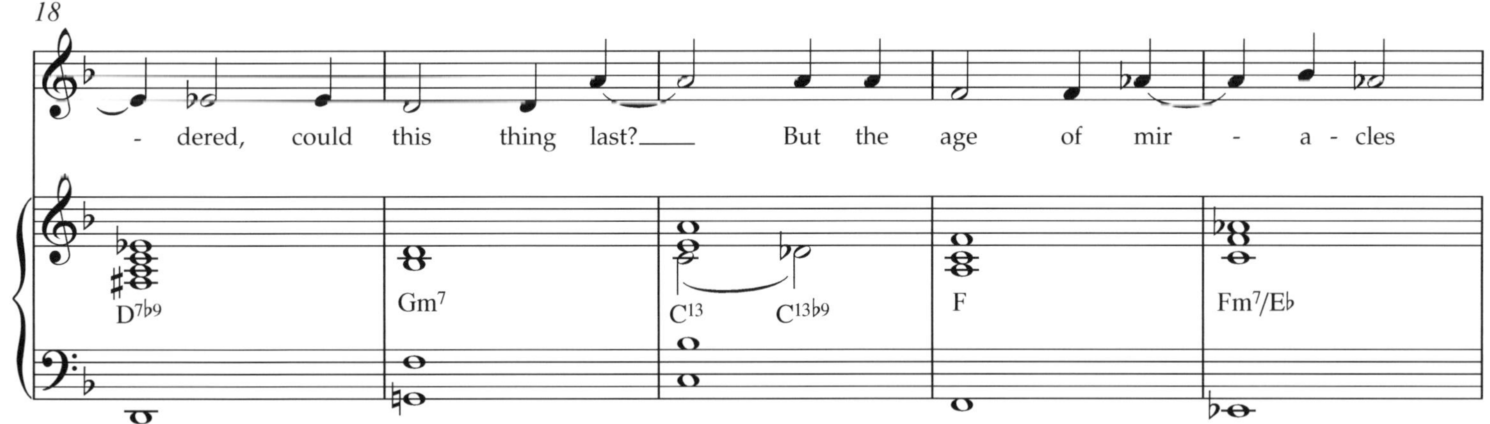

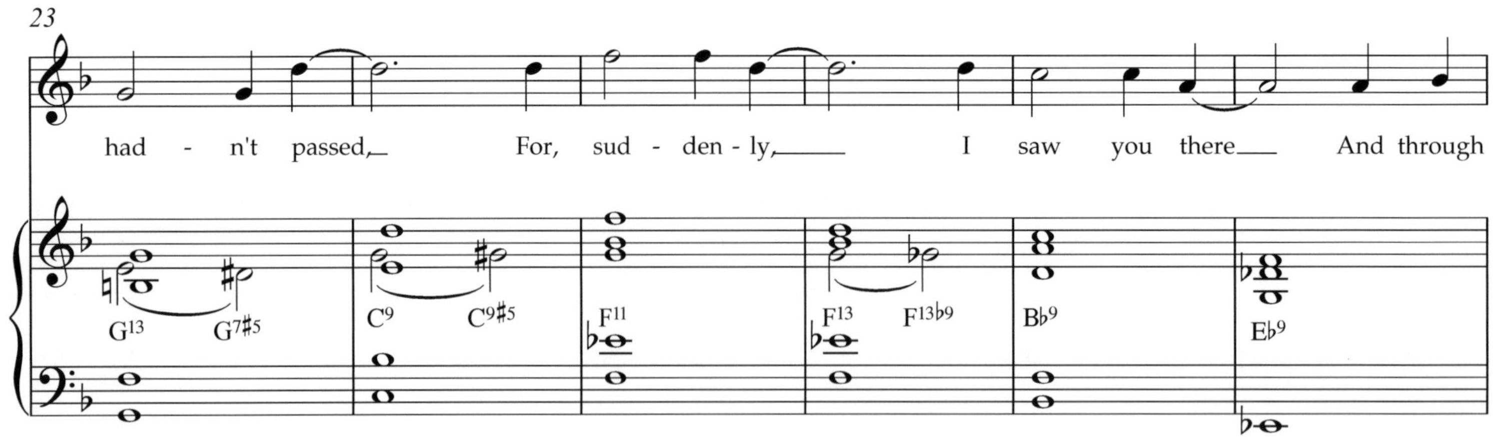

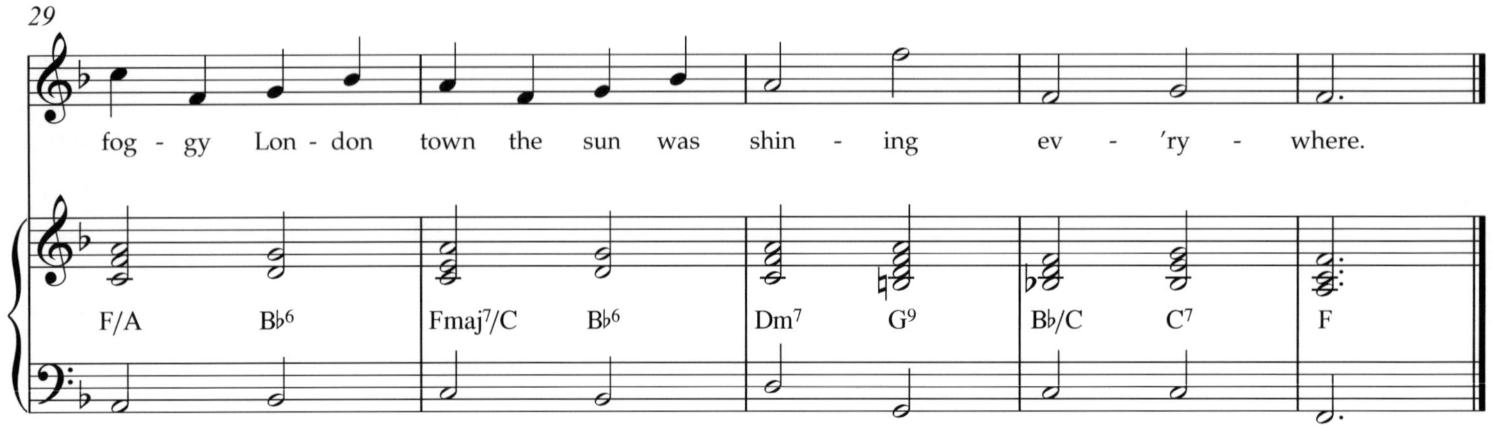

A FOGGY DAY
(SOLO ARRANGEMENT)

JUST ONE OF THOSE THINGS
(MELODY, LYRICS AND CHORD CHANGES)

Words and Music by
Cole Porter

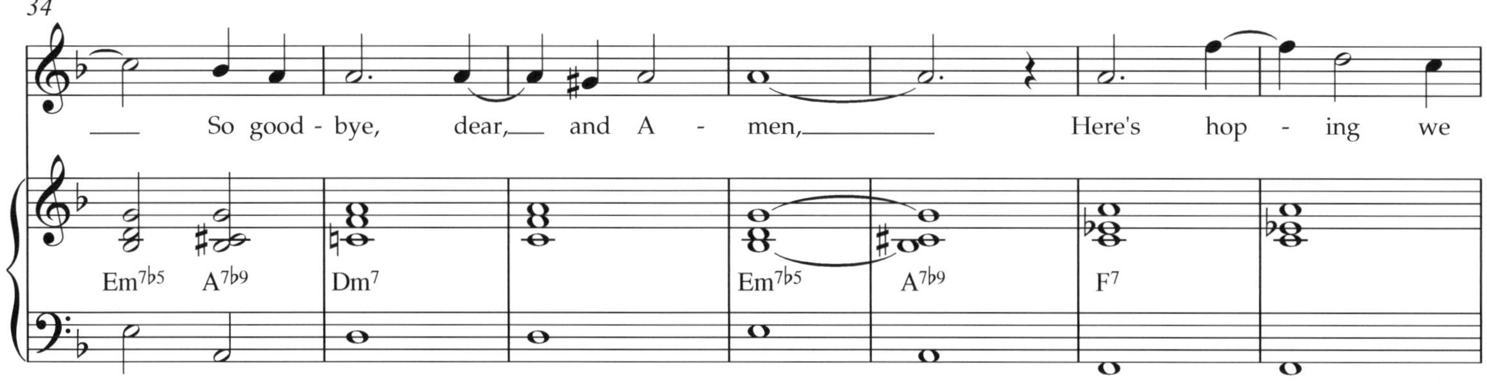

JUST ONE OF THOSE THINGS
(SOLO ARRANGEMENT)

THE SHADOW OF YOUR SMILE
(MELODY, LYRICS AND CHORD CHANGES)

Words by Paul Webster
Music by Johnny Mandel

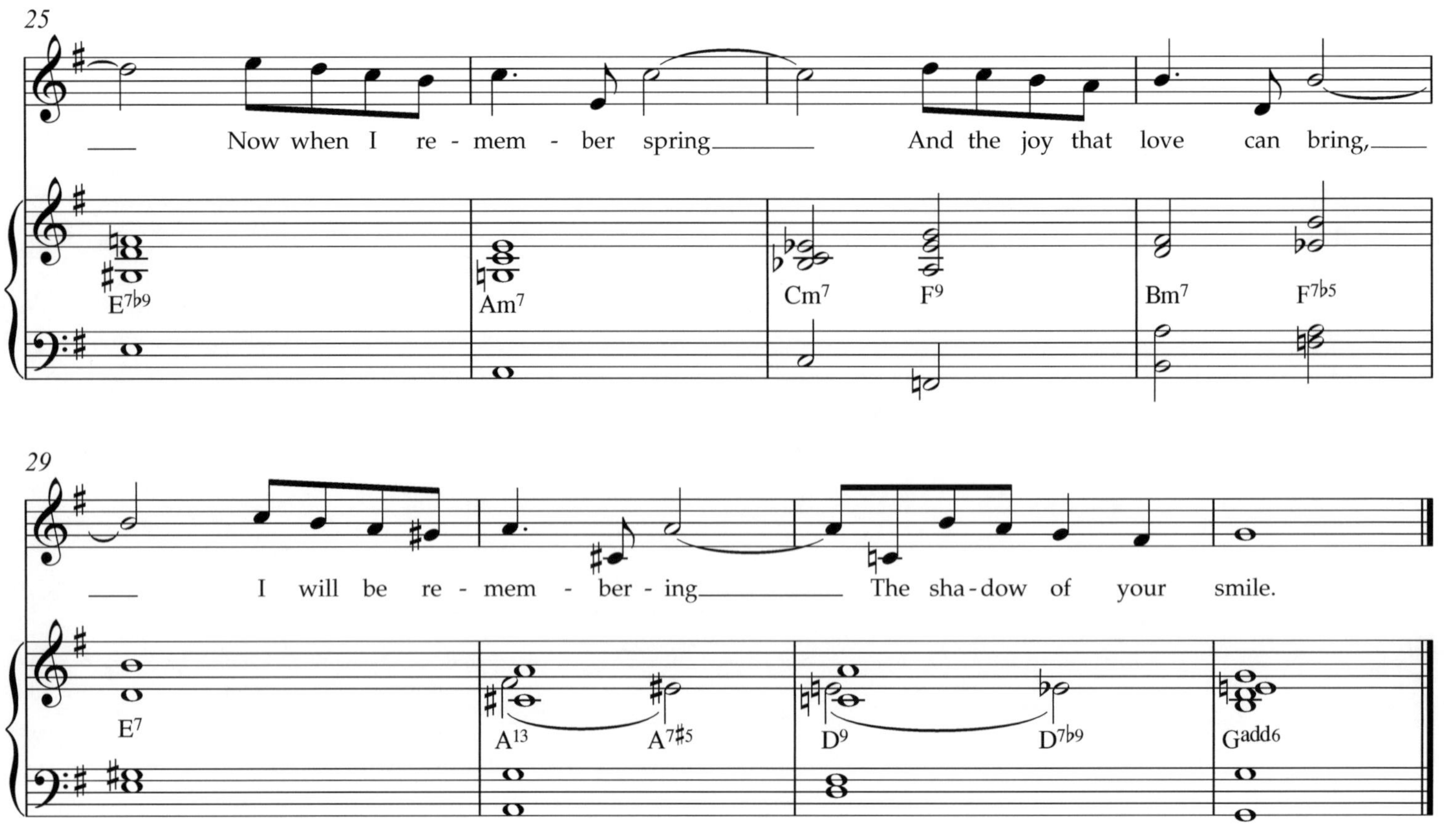

TRACK 6

THE SHADOW OF YOUR SMILE
(SOLO ARRANGEMENT)

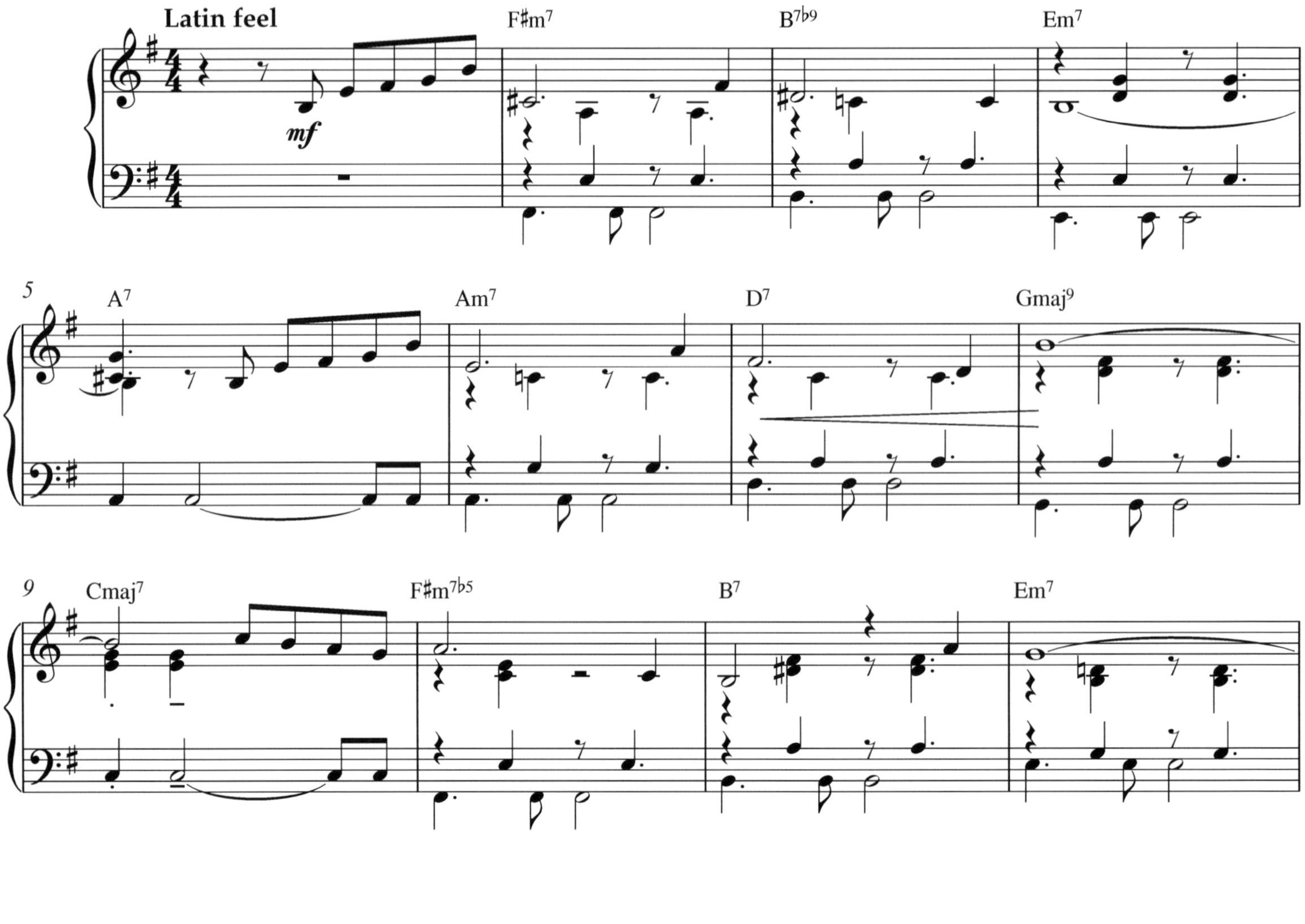

13
Em/D
C#m7b5
F#7
F#m7/B

17
B7
F#m7
B7
Em7

21
A7
Am7
D7
Bm7b5

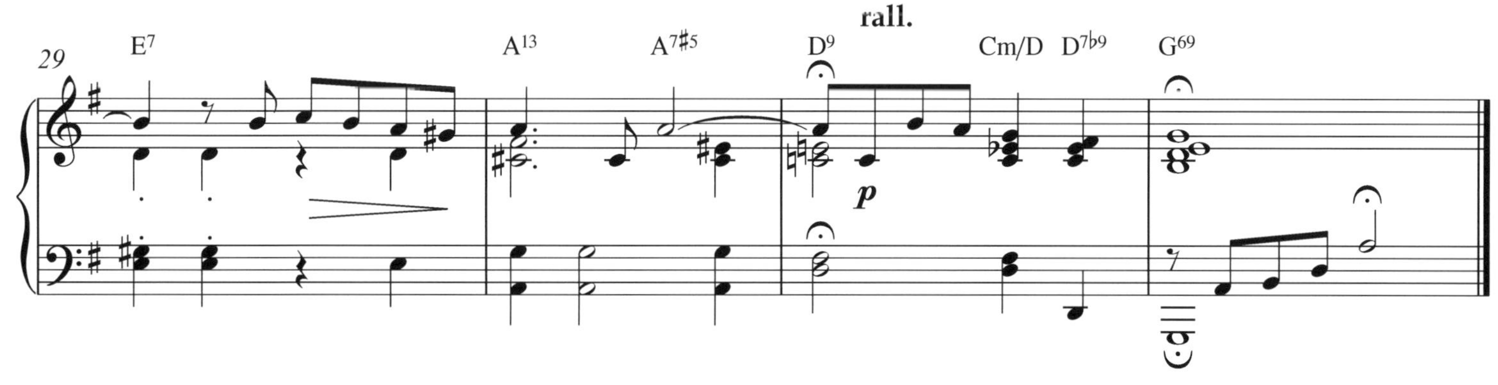
25
E7
Am7
Cm7
F7
Bm7
F7b5
rall.
29
E7
A13
A7#5
D9
Cm/D
D7b9
G69
p

FOLKS WHO LIVE ON THE HILL
(MELODY, LYRICS AND CHORD CHANGES)

Words by Oscar Hammerstein II
Music by Jerome Kern

And when the kids grow up and leave us, We'll sit and look at that same old view,
Dm7 G7#5 Cmaj7 C7 Fmaj7 G7 C/E Ebdim7
Just we two, Dar - by and Joan who used to be Jack and Jill,
Dm6 Am/C Em7 Am7 Dm7 G7#5 Cmaj7 C7
The folks that like to be called What they have al - ways been called
Fmaj7 G7 Em A7b5 Dm7 G7
'The folks who live on the hill'.
Em A7 D7 G7 C C7 Fm6 C

FOLKS WHO LIVE ON THE HILL

(SOLO ARRANGEMENT)

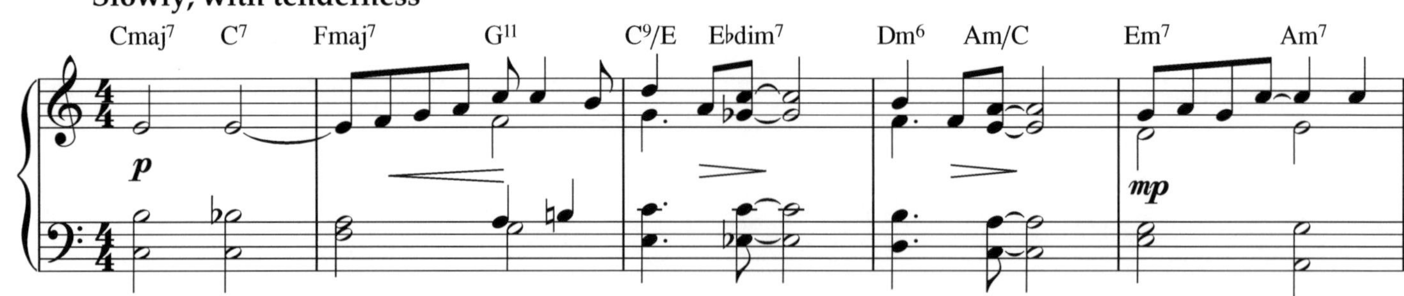

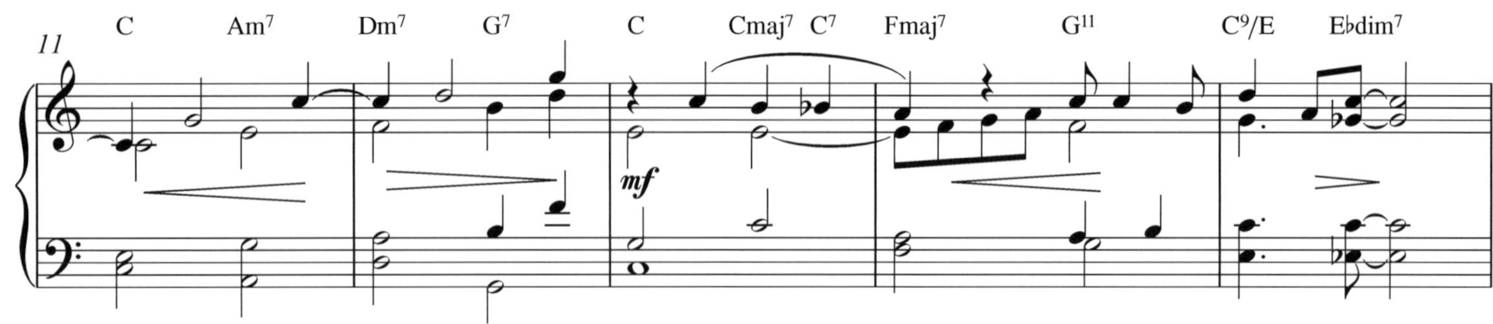

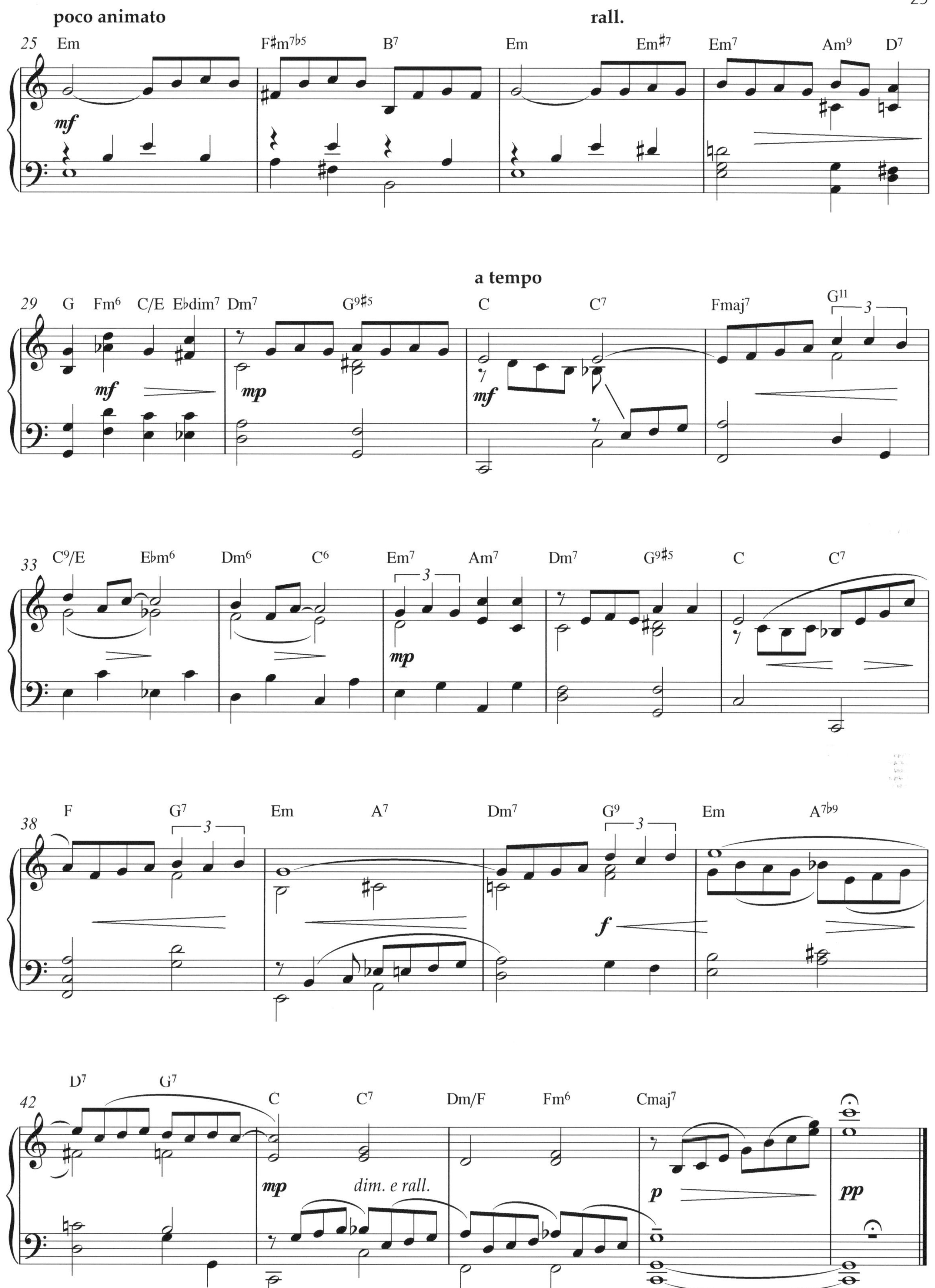
poco animato
rall.
a tempo
mf
mf
mp
mf
mp
mp
f
mp
dim. e rall.
p
pp

LET'S DO IT (LET'S FALL IN LOVE)

(MELODY, LYRICS AND CHORD CHANGES)

Words and Music by
Cole Porter

17
old Am - ster - dam do it, Not to men - tion the Fins.
eels, I might add, do it, Though it shocks 'em I know.
Gm7   Eb7   Dm7   Fm7   Bb7

21
Folks in Si - am do it, think of Si - am - ese twins. Some Ar - gen -
Why ask if shad do it, wait - er, bring me shad roe. In shal - low
Ebmaj7   Ab7   Dbmaj7   Cm11   F9

25
-tines, with - out means, do it, Peo - ple say in Bos - ton e - ven beans do it,
shoals Eng - lish soles do it, Gold - fish, in the priv - a - cy of bowls, do it,
Bb6   Cm7   F7   Bb6   Bb7   Eb7

29
Let's do it, let's fall in love. 2. Ro - man - tic love.
1.   2.
Bb6   Gm7   Cm7   F7   Bbmaj7   Cm7   F7   Bb

LET'S DO IT (LET'S FALL IN LOVE)

(SOLO ARRANGEMENT)

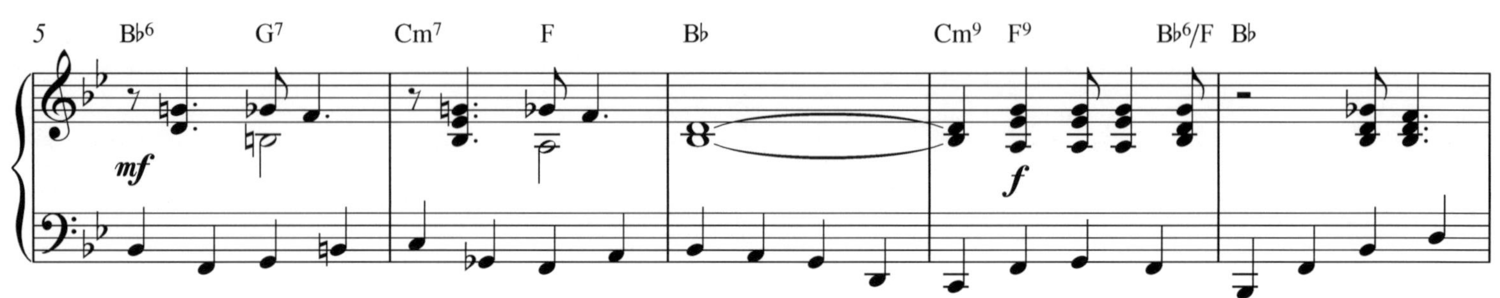

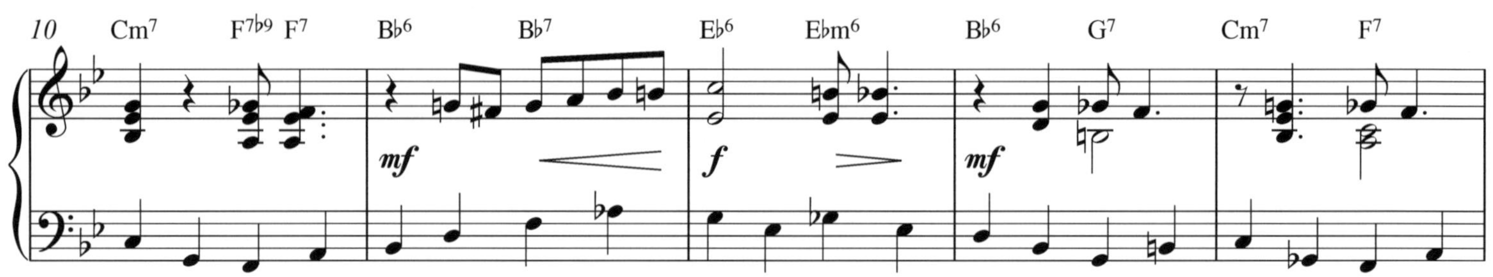

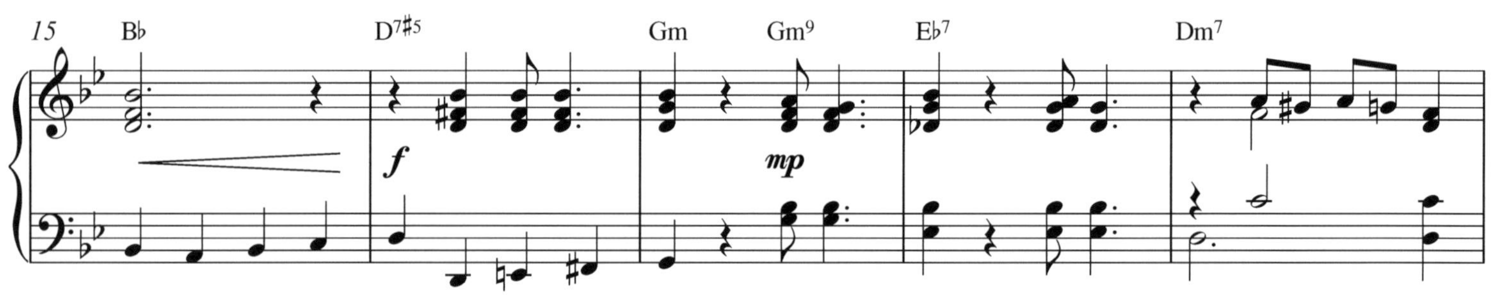

25
Bb6   Cm7   F   Bb6   Bb7   Eb7   Eb6 Eb7   Bb   Gm7
f

30
Cm7   F7   Bb   Gm7   Cm   F7   Bb6   Bb   Cm7   F7   Bb6   D/A Gm G/F
p leggiero

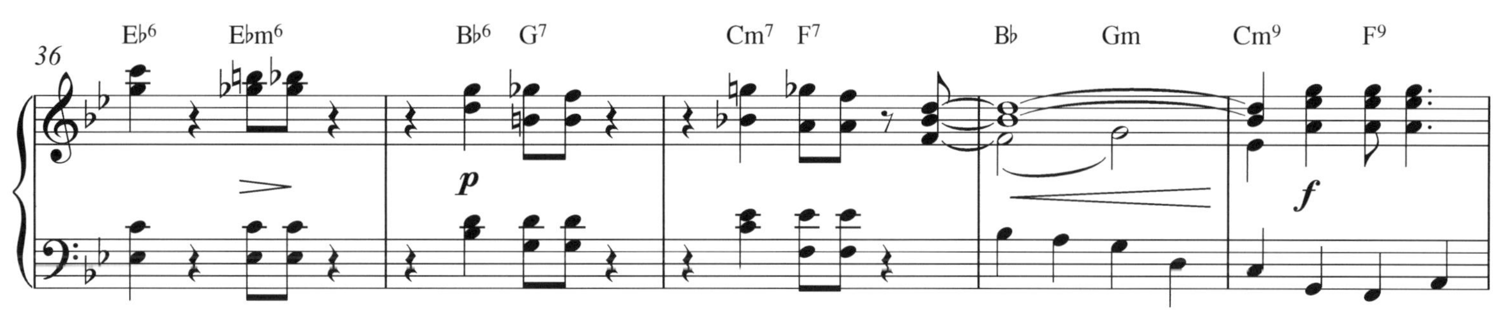
36
Eb6   Ebm6   Bb6   G7   Cm7   F7   Bb   Gm   Cm9   F9
p   f

41
Bb6   Bb   Cm7   F7   Bb6   Bb7   Eb6   Ebm6   Bb   Gm   Cm7   F13
f

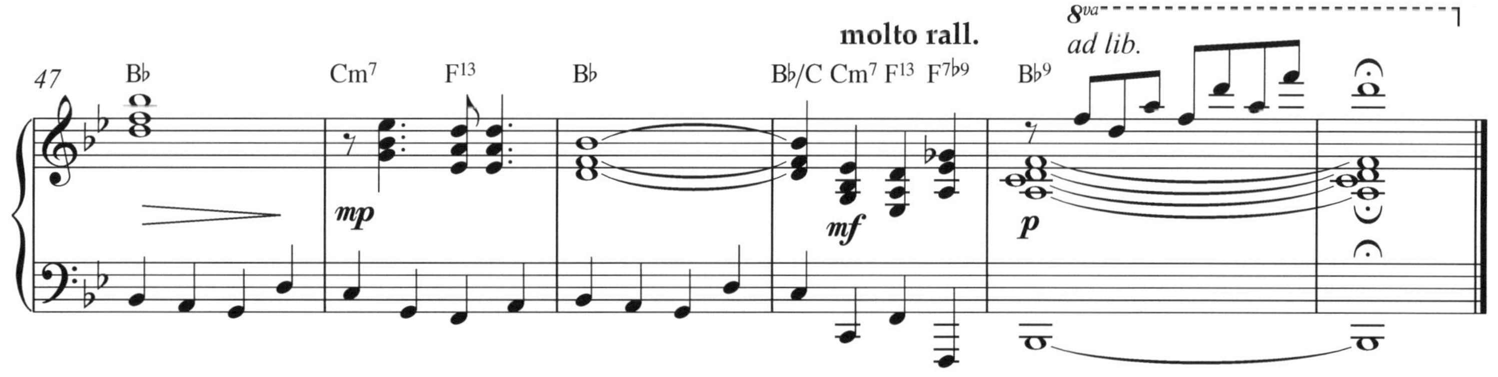
molto rall.
8va ad lib.
47
Bb   Cm7   F13   Bb   Bb/C Cm7 F13 F7b9   Bb9
mp   mf   p

LOVE IS HERE TO STAY

(MELODY, LYRICS AND CHORD CHANGES)

Words and Music by
George Gershwin and Ira Gershwin

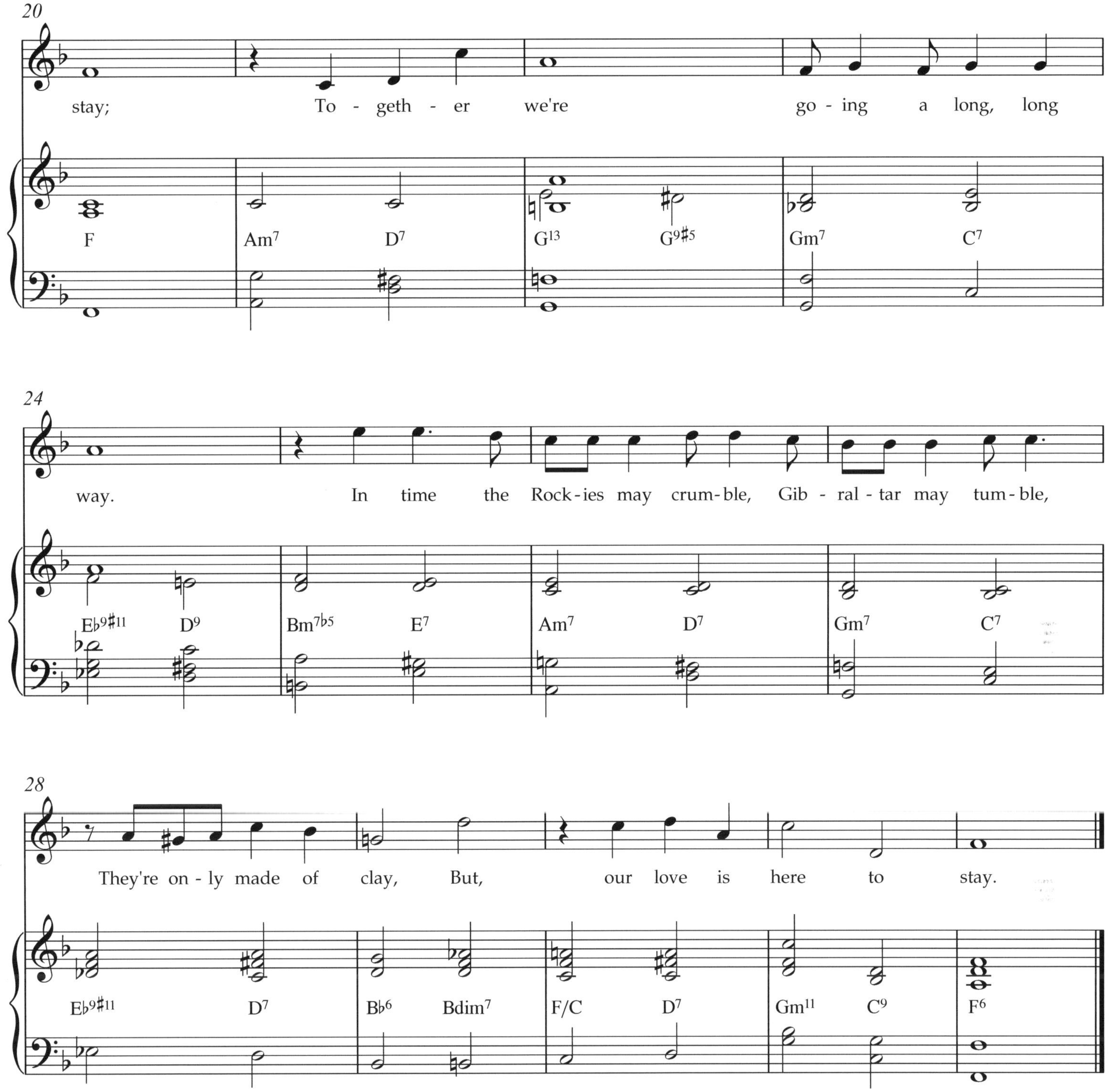

TRACK 9

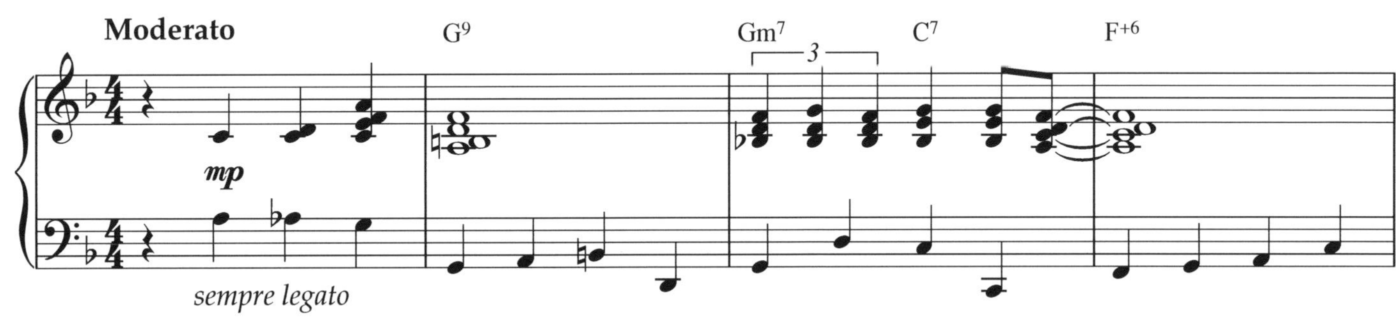

LOVE IS HERE TO STAY

(SOLO ARRANGEMENT)

molto rall.

I'VE GOT YOU UNDER MY SKIN
(MELODY, LYRICS AND CHORD CHANGES)

Words and Music by
Cole Porter

said to my-self, "This af-fair ne-ver will go so well." ________ But
Fm7b5 Fm7b5/Bb Bb7 D/Eb Ebmaj7 Eb6
why should I try to re-sist when, dar-ling, I know so well, ________ I've got you ________
Dm7 G7 B/C Cmaj7 C6 Fm7
________ un-der my skin. ________ I'd sac-ri-fice an-y-thing, come what might, For the
Bb11 Ebmaj7 Eb6 Fm7/Eb Bb7/Eb
sake of hav-in' you near, In spite of a warn-ing voice that comes in the night And re-
Ebmaj7 Eb7 Fm7/Eb Fm7b5/Eb

39
-peats and re-peats in my ear:_____ "Don't you know, lit-tle fool,_____ you nev-er can win?_____
Gm7 Gb7 F7(11) Bb13 Cm7 Fm7 Bb7#5 Ebmaj7
44
_____ Use your men-tal-i-ty,_____ wake up to re-al-i-ty."_____ But each
Gm7 Gbdim7 Fm9(11) Bb13 Ebmaj7 Bbm7 Eb7b9
49
time I do, just the thought of you Makes me stop, be-fore I be-gin, 'Cause I've
Ab6 Abm6 Eb6/Bb Gm7b5 C7b9
53
got you_____ un-der my skin. I've skin._____
1. 2.
Fm9(11) Bb13 Eb Gm7 C7b9 Eb Bb11 Eb

TRACK 10

I'VE GOT YOU UNDER MY SKIN
(SOLO ARRANGEMENT)

31
Eb   Fm7/Eb   Bb7/Eb   Ebmaj7
p
36
Eb7   Fm7/Eb   Fm7b5/Eb   Gm7   Gb7   F11   Bb7
41
Cm7   Fm7   Bb#5   Ebmaj7   Gm7   Gbdim7   Fm11   Bb13   Bb7
f
Held back
47
Ebmaj7   Bbm7   C7   Ab6   Abm6   Eb6/Bb
f   mf
a tempo
52
Gm7b5   C7b9   Fm9   Bb13   Eb   Cm7
mp   poco a poco dim.   p
57
Fm9   Bb13   Bb13b9   Eb   Ebmaj7
8vb loco   pp

THE VERY THOUGHT OF YOU
(MELODY, LYRICS AND CHORD CHANGES)

Words and Music by
Ray Noble

-dea of you, the long-ing here for you, You'll ne-ver know how slow the
Ab   Ab6   Abmaj7 Bbm7
mo - ments go till I'm near to you, I see your face in ev - 'ry
Bdim7 Cm6 Bb9   Bbm7 Eb7
flow - er, Your eyes in stars a - bove, It's just the thought of you, The ve - ry
Gm7b5 C7 Fm Fm/Eb Ddim7 G7 Cm7 F7
thought of you, my love. The ve - ry love.
Bbm7 Eb7 Ab Ab6 Bbm7 Eb7 Ab

THE VERY THOUGHT OF YOU
(SOLO ARRANGEMENT)

TRACK 11

Ab6
Ab Bbm7 Bdim7 Fm7/C
mf cresc.
Bb9
Cm Bbm11 Eb7 Gm7b5 C7
f mf
Fm Bb9 Dm7b5 G Cm7 F7
p
1.
Bbm7 Eb7 Ab Bbm7 Eb13
mf mp
2.
Abmaj7
Bbm7 Eb13 Ab Abadd 9
pp pp

for Thelma

ALL THE THINGS YOU ARE

(MELODY, LYRICS AND CHORD CHANGES)

Words by Oscar Hammerstein II
Music by Jerome Kern

Moderato – legato e sostenuto

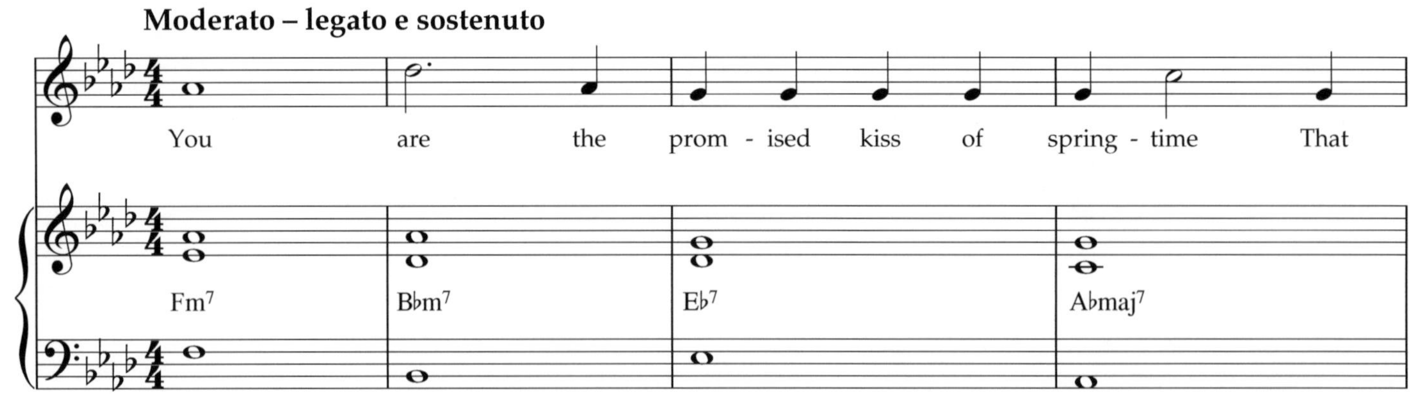

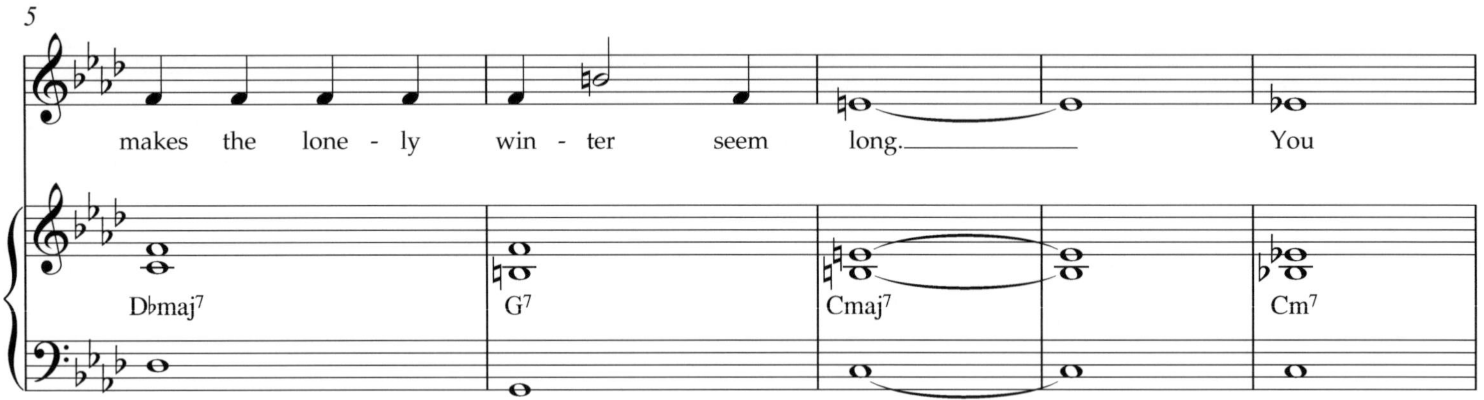

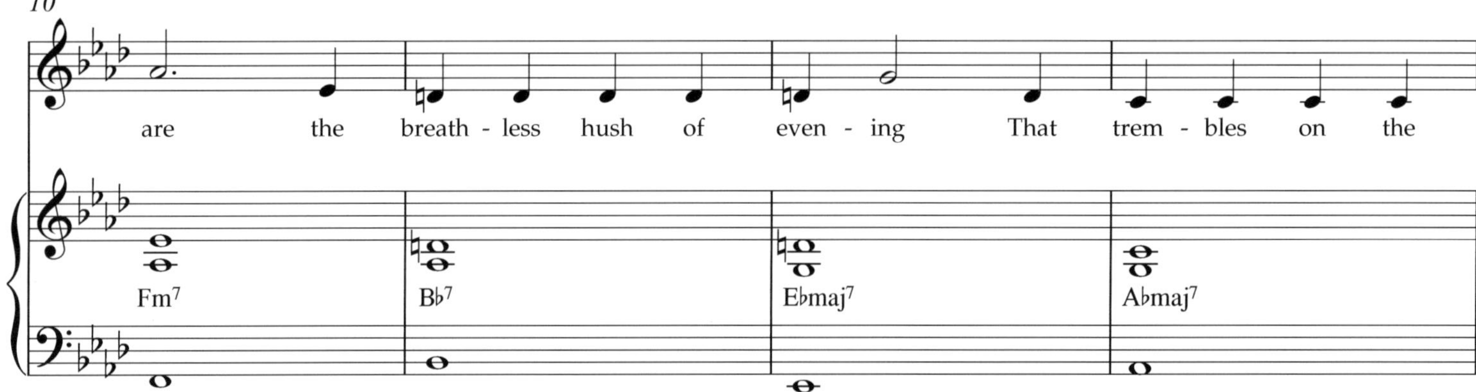

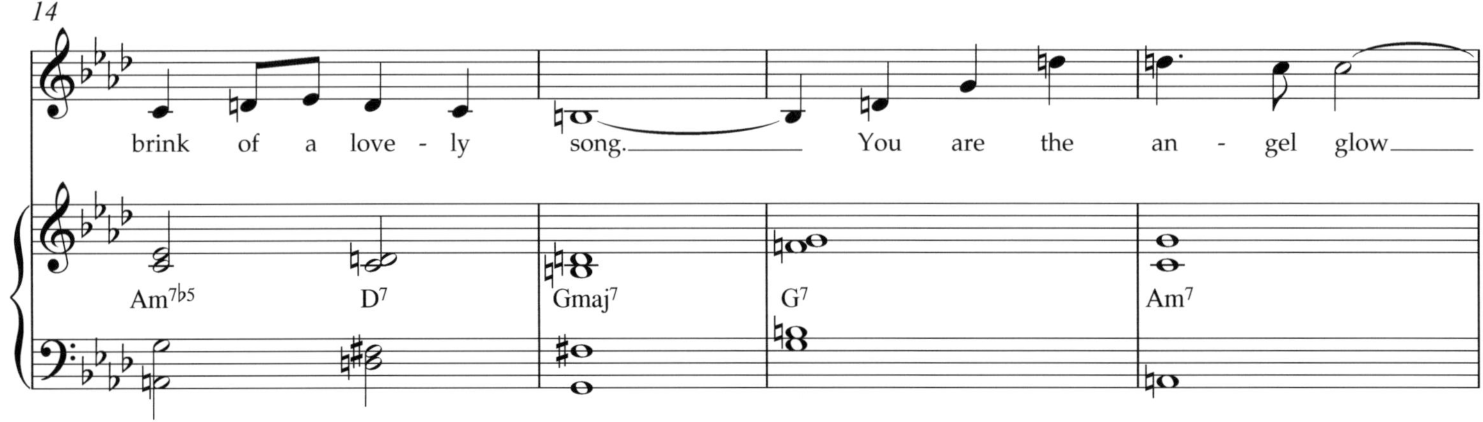

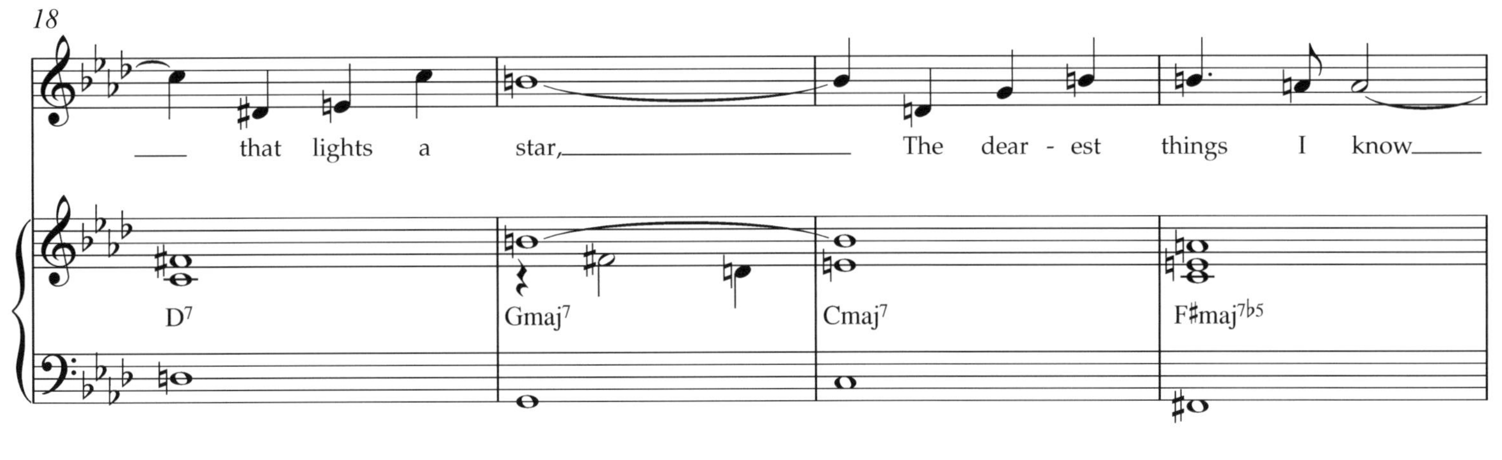
18
that lights a star, The dear-est things I know
D7
Gmaj7
Cmaj7
F#maj7b5

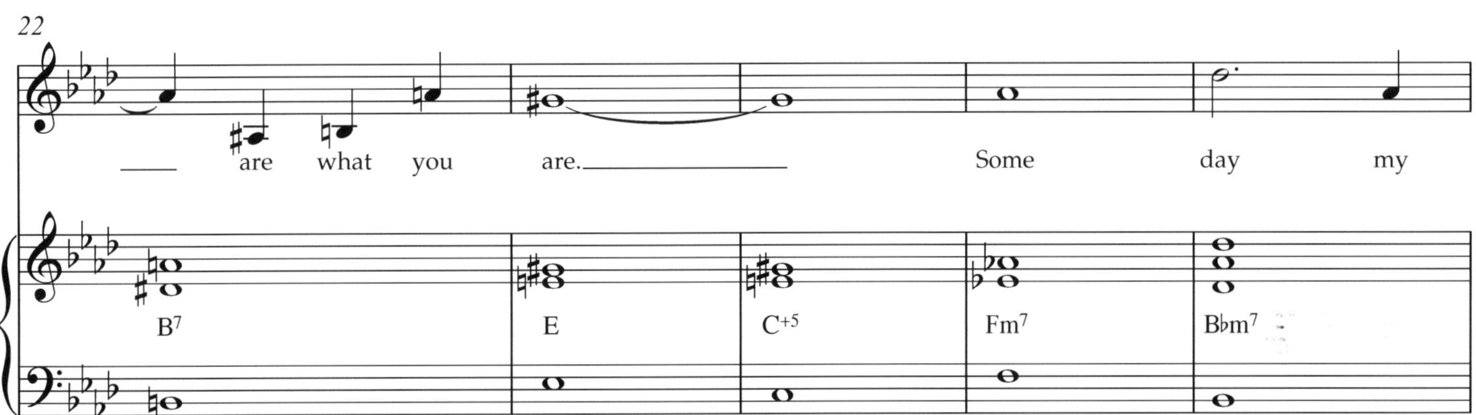
22
are what you are. Some day my
B7
E
C+5
Fm7
Bbm7

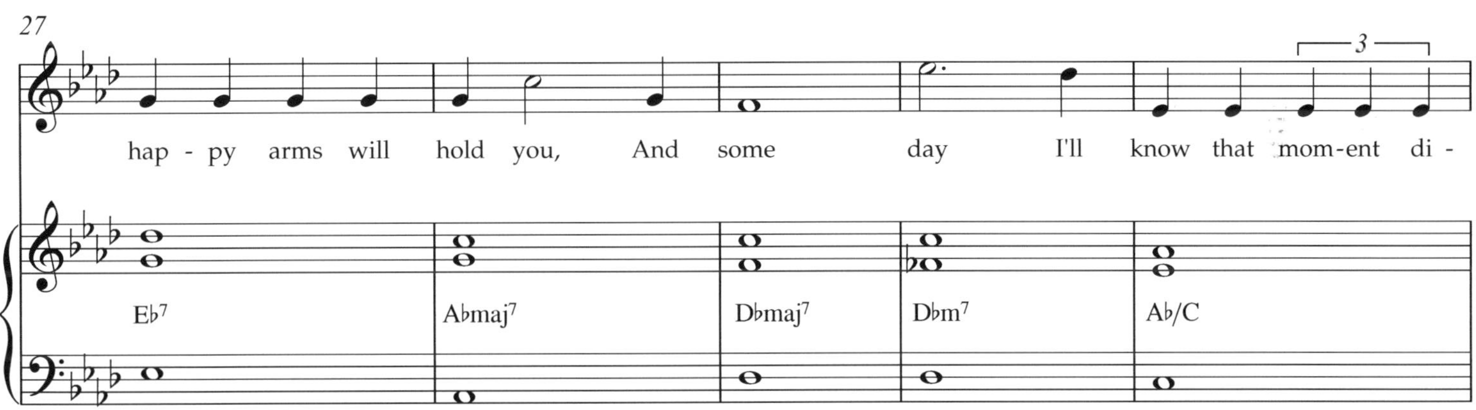
27
3
hap-py arms will hold you, And some day I'll know that mom-ent di-
Eb7
Abmaj7
Dbmaj7
Dbm7
Ab/C

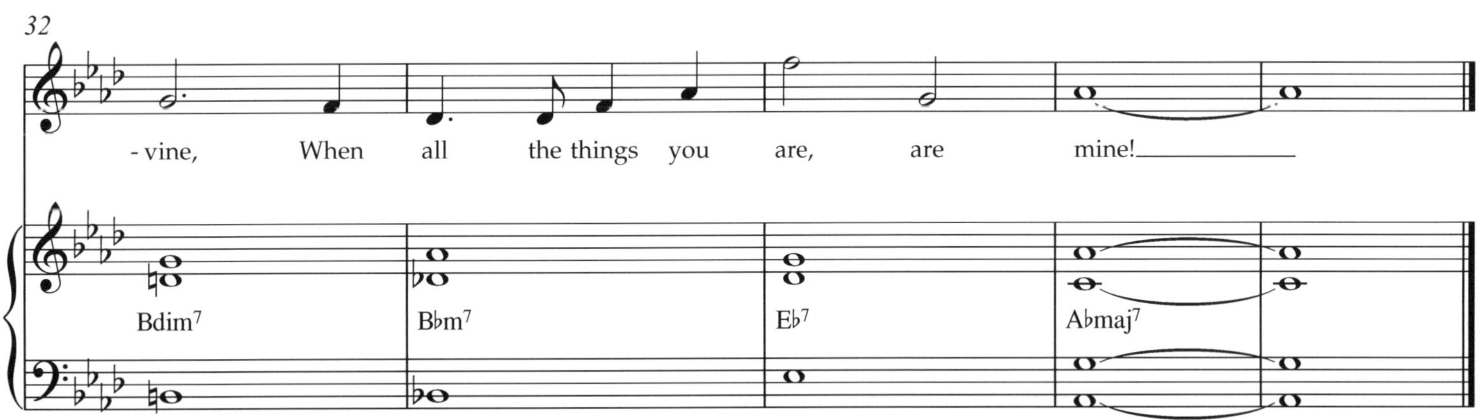
32
-vine, When all the things you are, are mine!
Bdim7
Bbm7
Eb7
Abmaj7

for Thelma

ALL THE THINGS YOU ARE
(SOLO ARRANGEMENT)

Moderato – legato e sostenuto

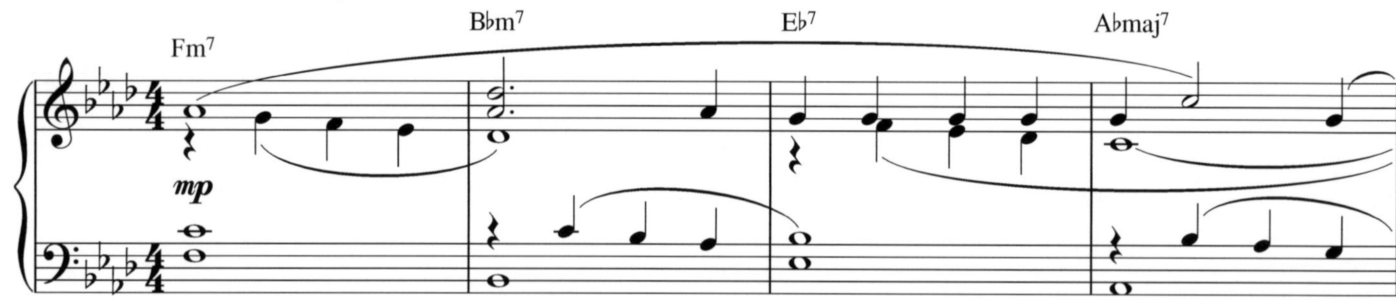

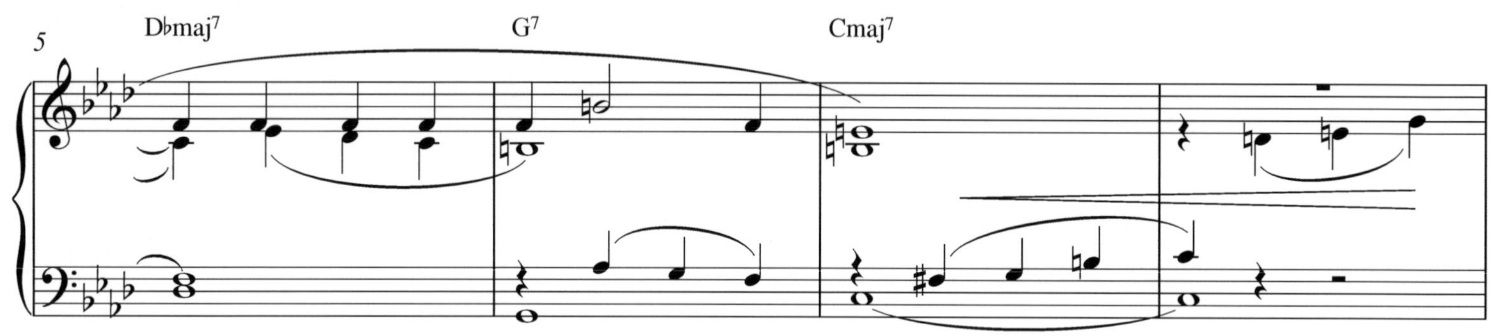

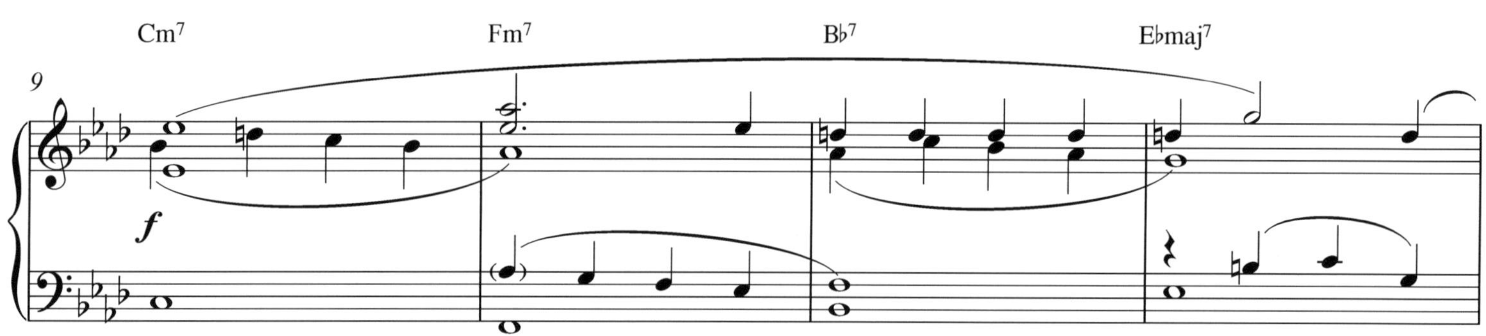

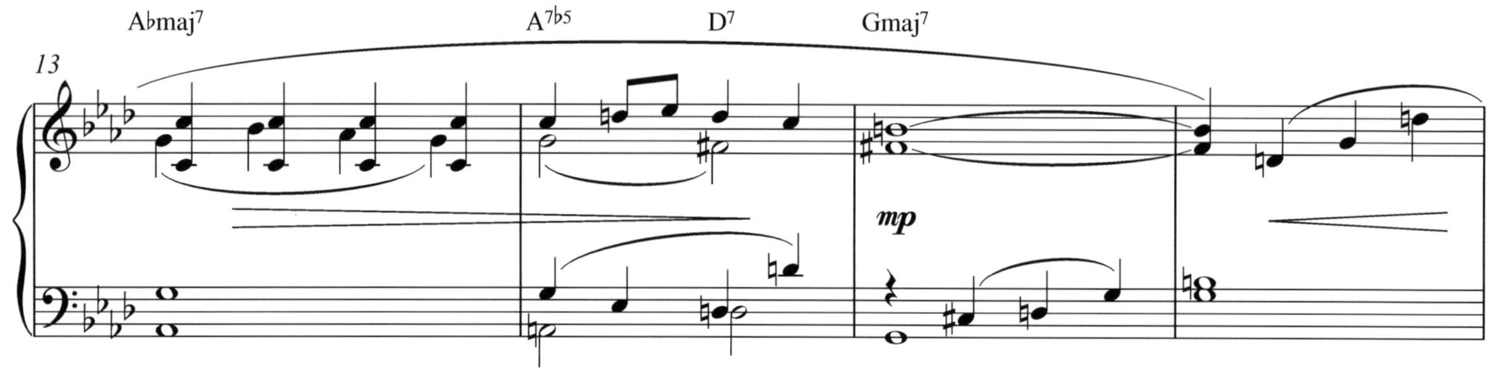

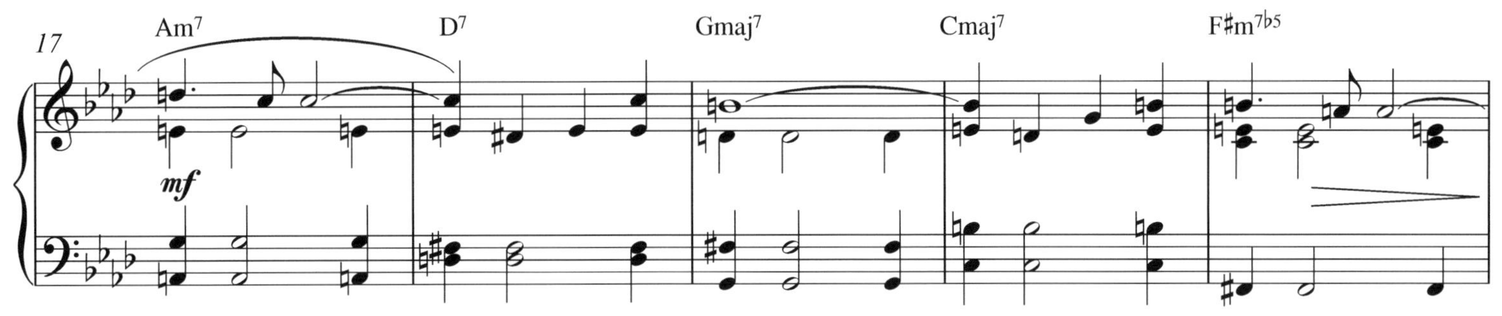
17
Am7   D7   Gmaj7   Cmaj7   F#m7b5
mf

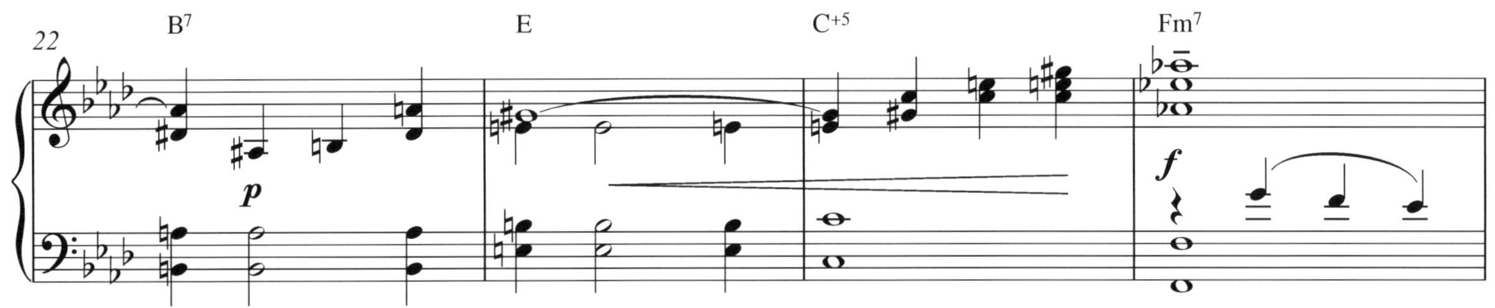
22
B7   E   C+5   Fm7
p   f

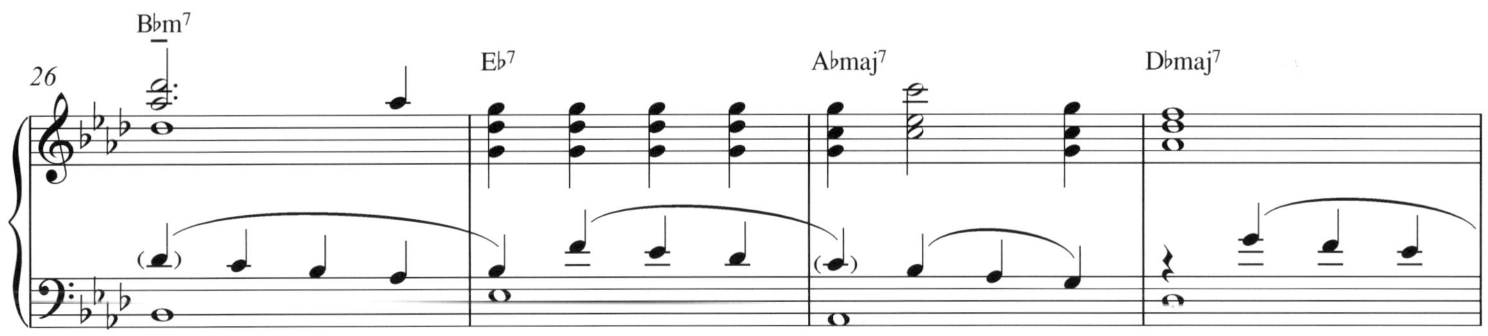
26
Bbm7   Eb7   Abmaj7   Dbmaj7

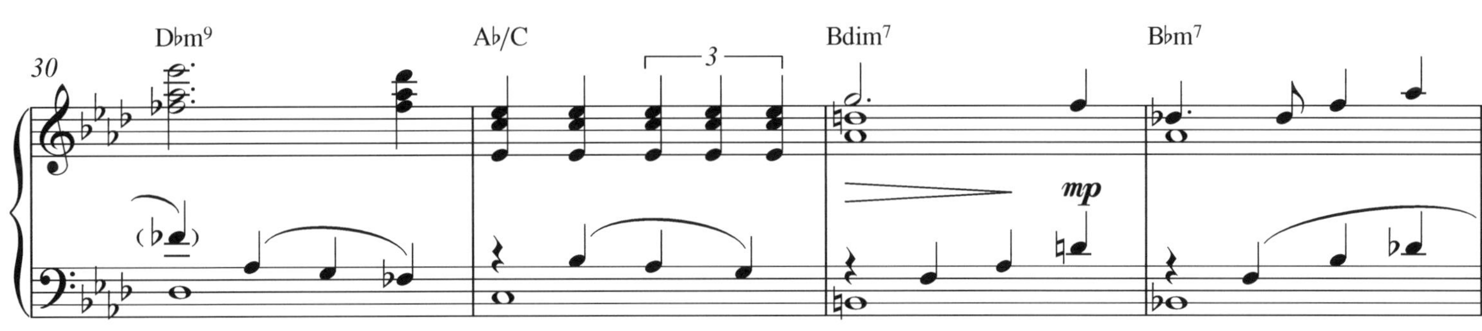
30
Dbm9   Ab/C   3   Bdim7   Bbm7
mp

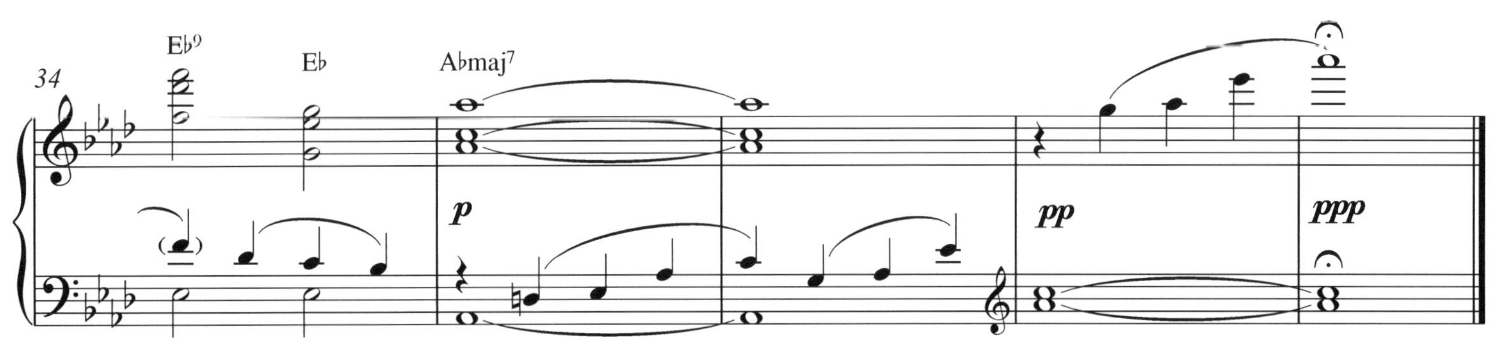
34
Eb9   Eb   Abmaj7
p   pp   ppp

I'VE GOT THE WORLD ON A STRING

(MELODY, LYRICS AND CHORD CHANGES)

Words by Ted Koehler
Music by Harold Arlen

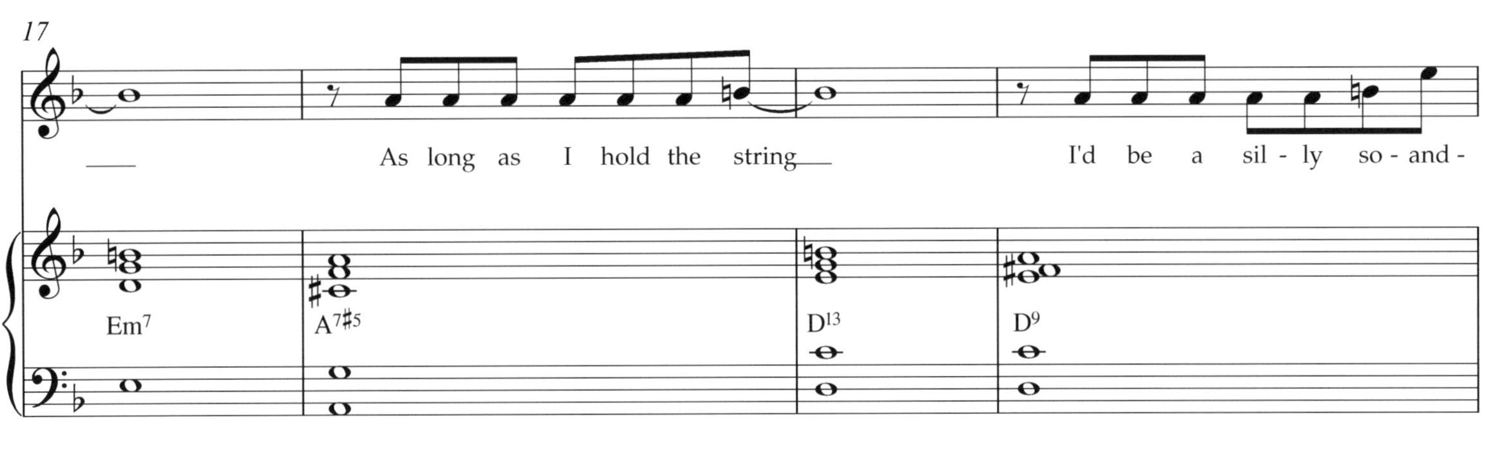
17
As long as I hold the string I'd be a sil - ly so - and -
Em7 A7#5 D13 D9

21
-so, If I should e - ver let go I've got the
G13 G7#5 Gm9 C13

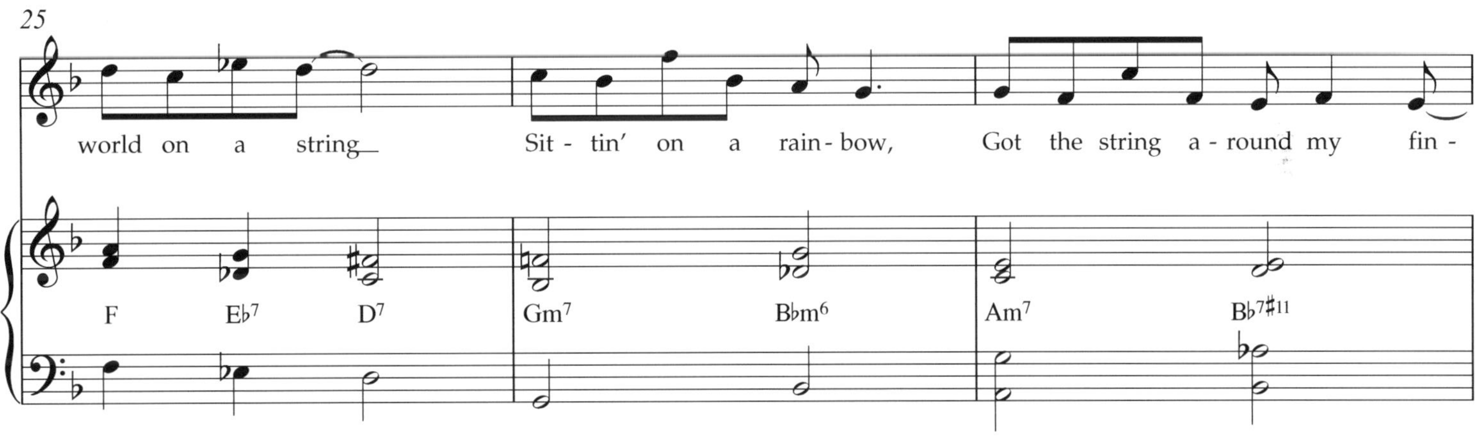
25
world on a string Sit - tin' on a rain - bow, Got the string a - round my fin -
F Eb7 D7 Gm7 Bbm6 Am7 Bb7#11

28
- ger, What a world, what a life — I'm in love!
Am7 D7b9 Gm7 C7 Gm11 C9 F6

TRACK 13

I'VE GOT THE WORLD ON A STRING
(SOLO ARRANGEMENT)

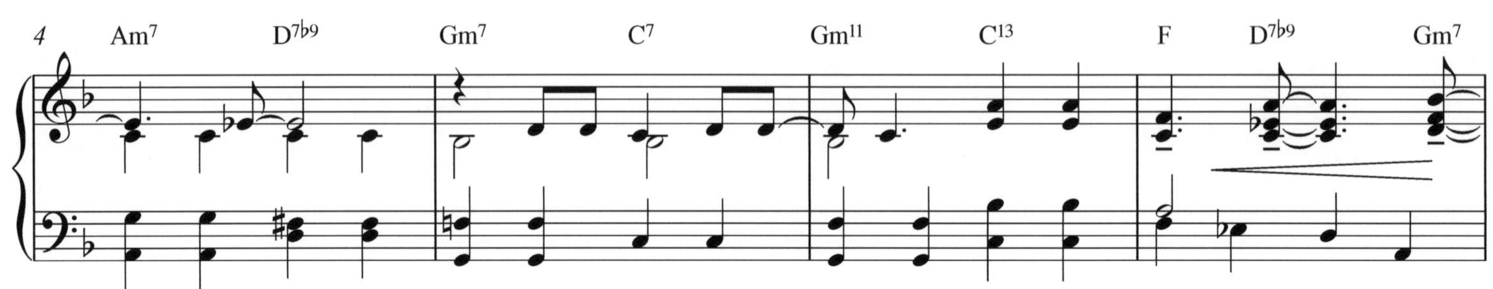

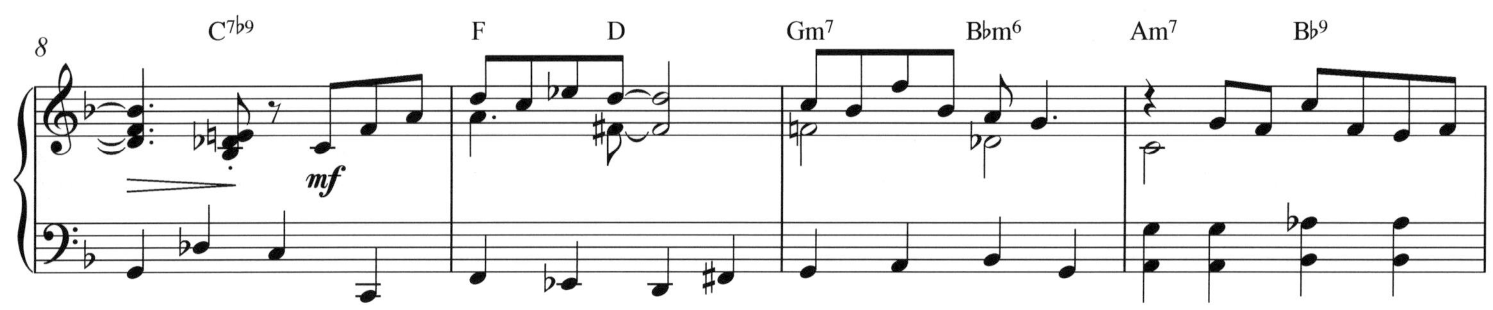

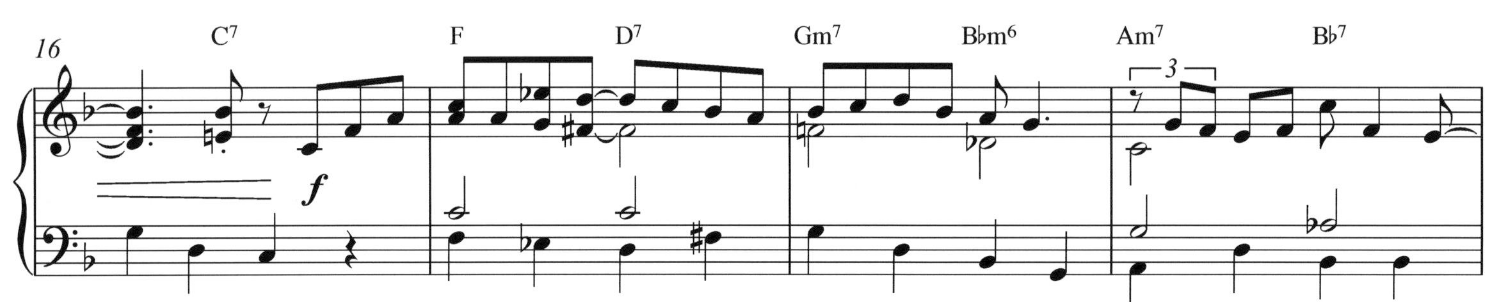

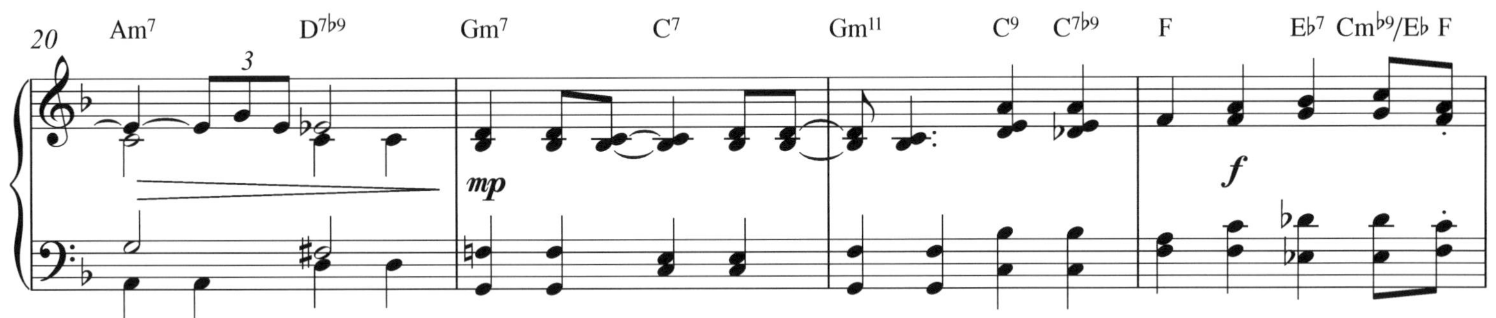

20
Am7   D7b9   Gm7   C7   Gm11   C9   C7b9   F   Eb7   Cmb9/Eb   F
3
mp
f

24
Em7   A9#5   D13   D9
mf

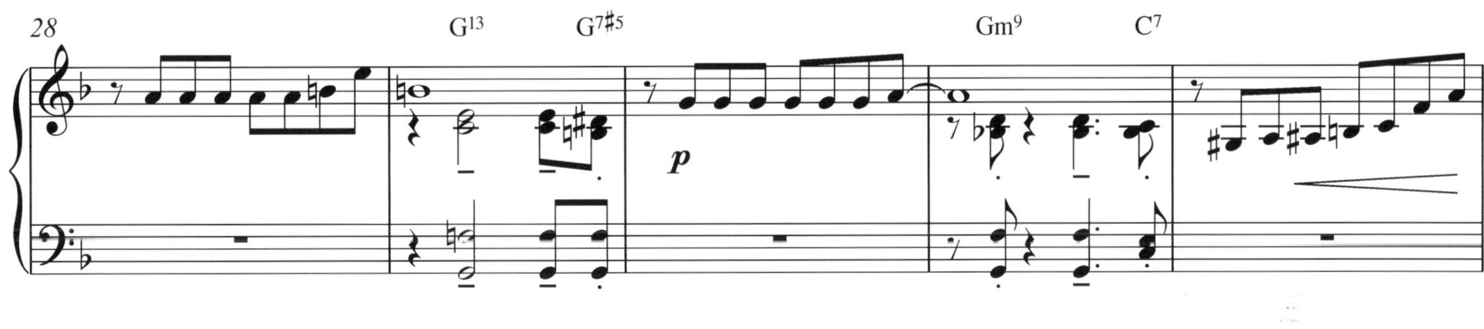

28
G13   G7#5   Gm9   C7
p

33
F   Eb7   D7   Gm7   Gm7b5   Bbm6   Am7   Bb7#11   Am7   D7b9
3
mf

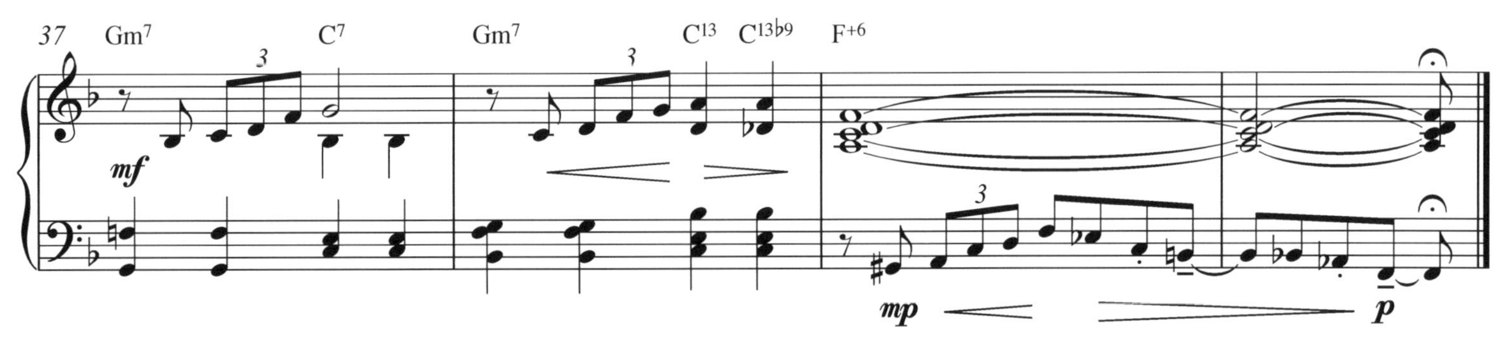

37
Gm7   C7   Gm7   C13   C13b9   F+6
3   3
mf
3
mp   p

THEY CAN'T TAKE THAT AWAY FROM ME

(MELODY, LYRICS AND CHORD CHANGES)

Words and Music by
George Gershwin and Ira Gershwin

We may ne - ver, ne - ver meet a - gain On the bump - y road to
Am7 Adim/D Gm7 Am7 D7 Gm7 Am7 D7 Gm7 Em7b5 A7#5
love. Still I'll al - ways, al - ways keep the mem - r'y of The way you hold your knife,
Am9 D7 Gm7 Am7b5 D7b9 Gm7 C7 Eb/F F7 Bb11
The way we danced till three, The way you changed my life.
Ebmaj7 Fm7 Gm7 Gbdim7 Fm11 Bb11
No, no! They can't take that a - way from me! No! They
Bbm7 Eb7 Abmaj7 Fm7 Bb7 Cm Fm7b5(sus)

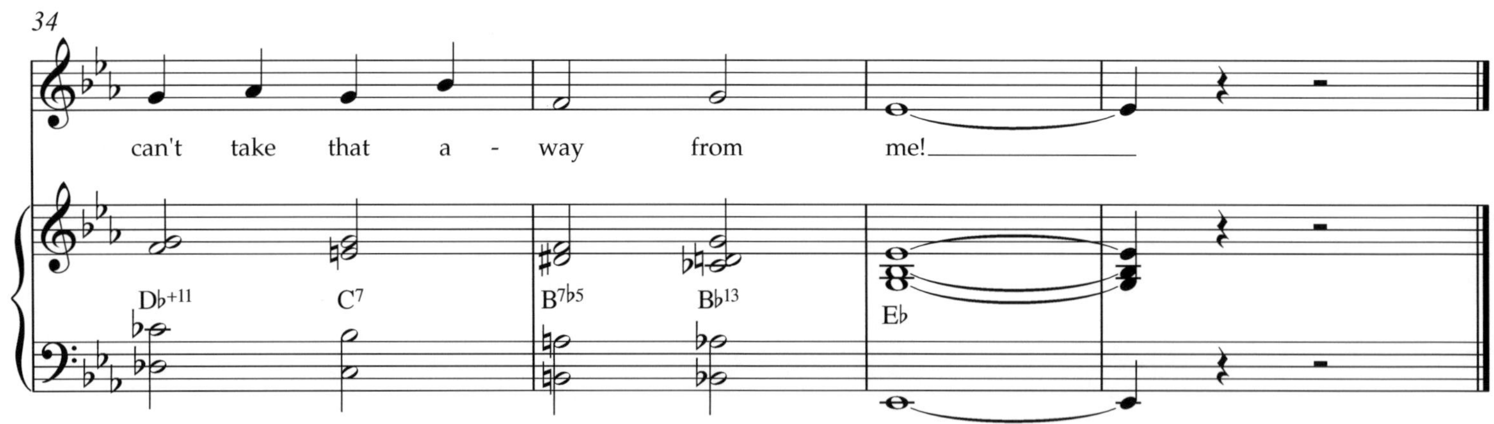

TRACK 14

THEY CAN'T TAKE THAT AWAY FROM ME

(SOLO ARRANGEMENT)

Medium swing

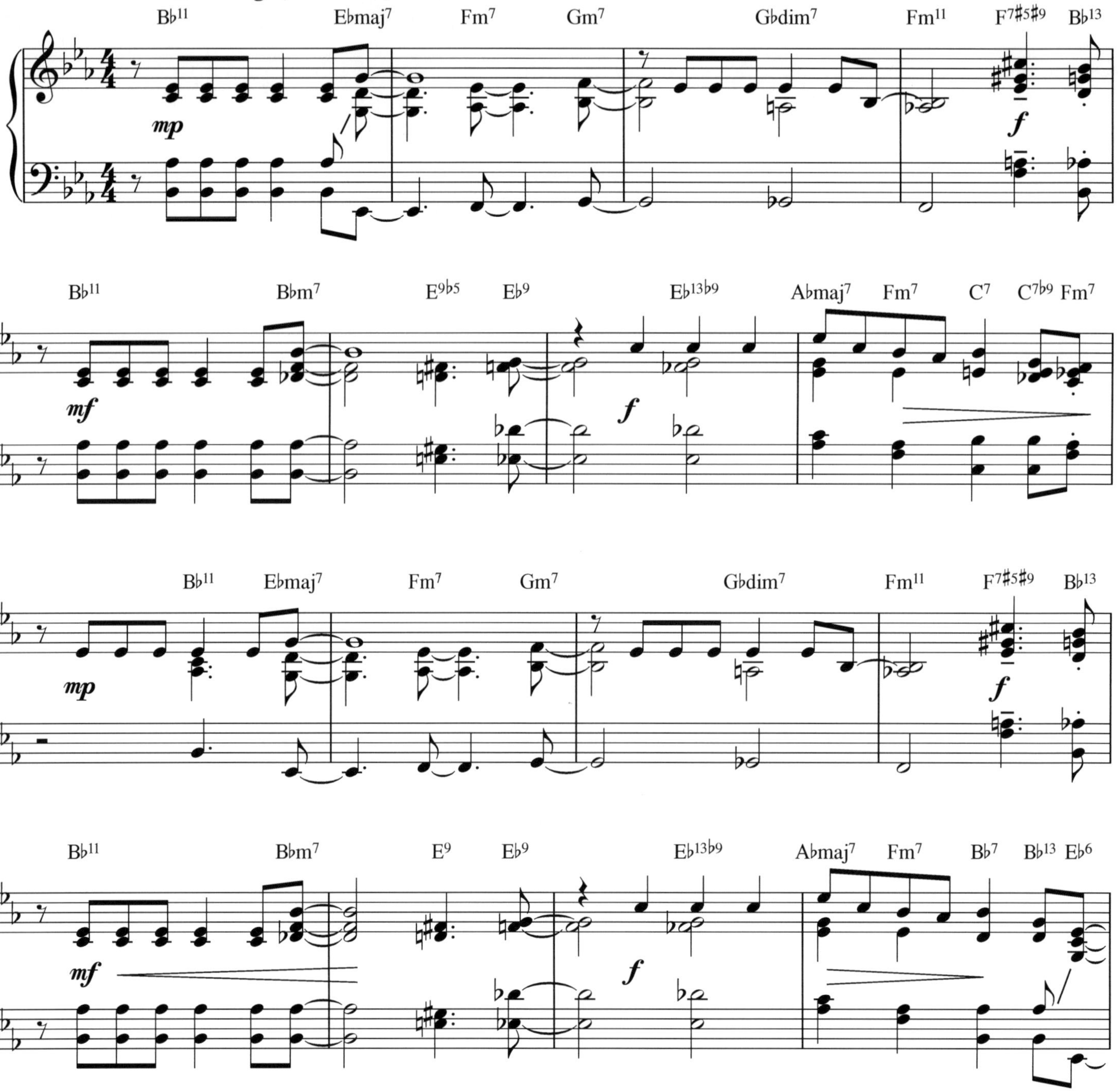

STORMY WEATHER
(MELODY, LYRICS AND CHORD CHANGES)
Words by Ted Koehler
Music by Harold Arlen
Slow swing
Don't know why there's no sun up in the sky, Stor-my wea-ther.
Since my man and I ain't to-ge-ther, Keeps rain-in' all the time.
Life is bare, gloom and mis-'ry ev-'ry-where Stor-my wea-ther.
Just can't get my poor self to-ge-ther, I'm wea-ry all the time.

So wea-ry all the time. When he went a-way the blues walked in and met me. If he stays a-way old rock-in' chair will get me. All I do is pray the Lord a-bove will let me Walk in the sun once more. Can't go on, ev'-ry-thing I had is gone, Stor-my wea-ther. Since my man and I ain't to-ge-ther,
Am7 D7b9 G C G C G C G G G/B Bb7b5 Am7 D7b9 G G#dim7 Am7 D7b9#5 G Am7 D9 G G7

TRACK 15

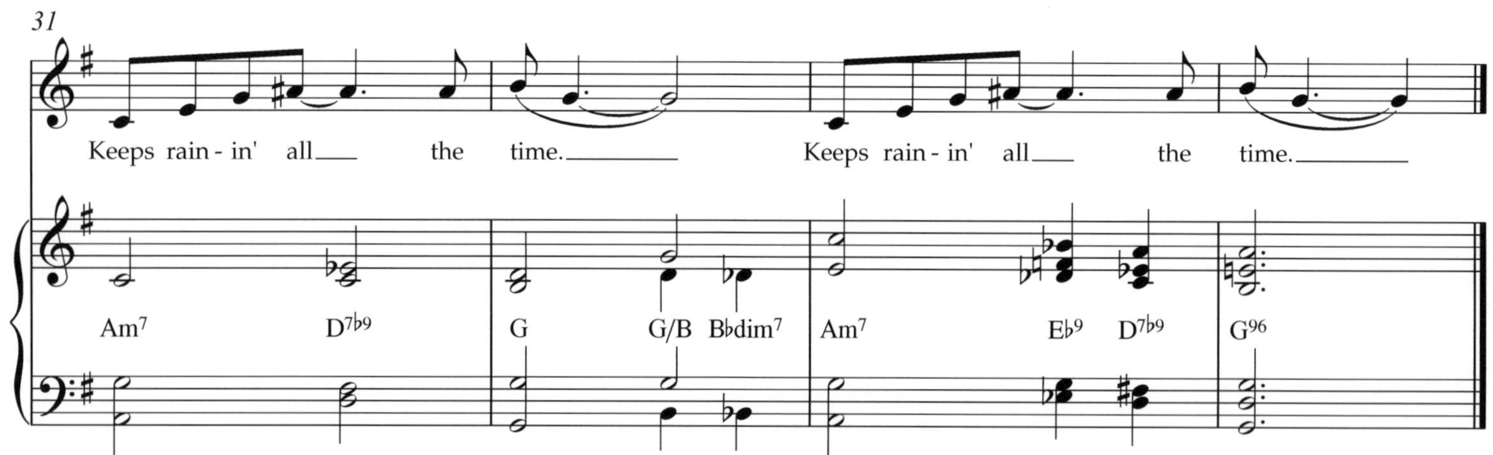

STORMY WEATHER

(SOLO ARRANGEMENT)

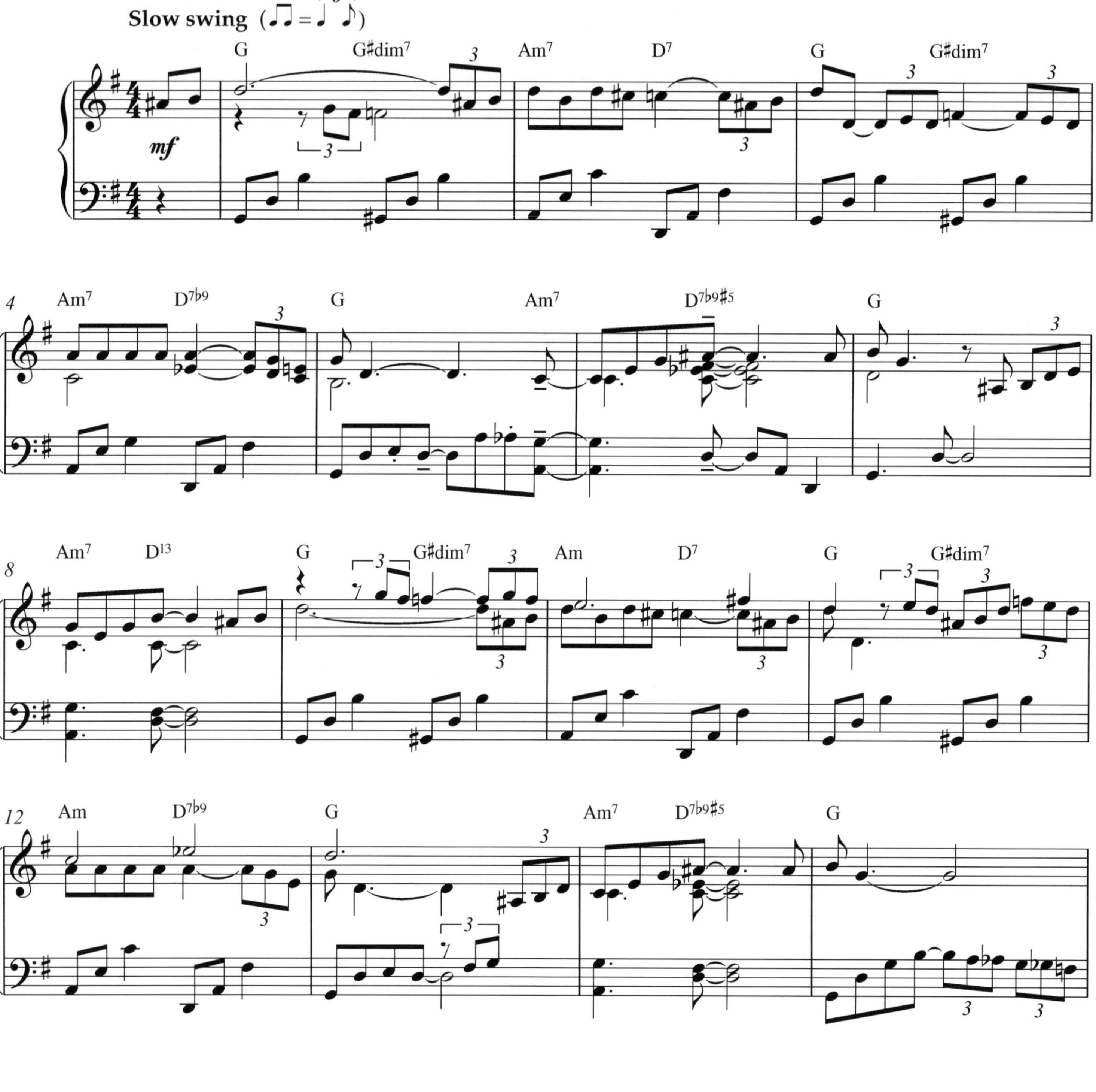

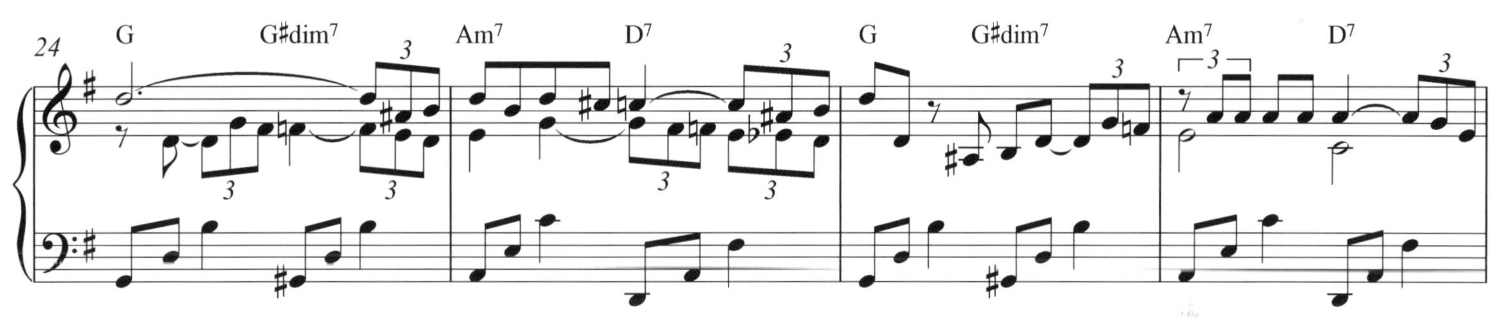

for Laura and Simon

LAURA
(MELODY, LYRICS AND CHORD CHANGES)

Words by Johnny Mercer
Music by David Raksin

Those eyes, how fam-il-iar they seem. She gave your ve-ry first
kiss to you, That was Lau - ra, but she's on-ly a dream.
for Laura and Simon
LAURA
(SOLO ARRANGEMENT)
TRACK 16
Tenderly
mp
mf
cresc.
p
f